ANTONY PRESTON

FIGHTING SHIPS OF WORLD WAR 3

ANTONY PRESTON

FIGHTING SHIPS OF WORLD WAR 3

HAMLYN
London · New York · Sydney · Toronto
A Bison Book

Distributed by
The Hamlyn Publishing Group
London – New York – Sydney – Toronto
Astronaut House, Feltham
Middlesex, England.

Published by
Bison Books Corp
17 Sherwood Place
Greenwich CT 06830
USA

ISBN 0 600 38488 8
Printed in Hong Kong

Page 1: Sikorsky CH-53E Super Stallion, latest version of the US Navy and Marine Corps assault transport helicopter.
Page 2-3: The battleship USS *New Jersey* seen in 1983 shortly after she recommissioned with an updated missile armament. Her escort is the *Knox* class frigate *Meyer Kord*.
This page: The British nuclear-powered attack submarine HMS *Trafalgar*.

CONTENTS

HMS *Brilliant*, a British Type 22 ship seen during her trials, a typical antisubmarine frigate designed to work in mid-ocean.

1. NAVAL POWER AND TECHNOLOGY

The whole nature of naval warfare has changed since the end of World War II, and today, as people begin to think the unthinkable, it is hard for the layman to understand such radical changes. Possession of a tiny 'black box' can nullify the most imposing weapons, while lack of it can leave one defenseless. Each year weapons increase in destructive power and their cost spirals upward. Nowhere is this trend more noticeable than in navies, whose imposing ships cost hundreds of millions and yet can apparently be sunk by a single missile.

When World War II ended the ferment in naval technology was just beginning. There were, as always, two schools of thought: those who believed that navies had a future and those who thought that air power, and in particular nuclear weapons had made sea power obsolete. The navalist had accepted the demise of the battleship as long ago as 1941 but said that the aircraft carrier was the new capital ship. The air power extremists, in contrast, claimed that 'the Bomb' needed only a long range aircraft to deliver it.

The air power lobby seemed to be winning the game when in 1949 Congress was persuaded to veto US Navy plans to build a large aircraft carrier, the *United States*, in favor of B-36 bombers. Fortunately the Korean War showed just how valuable aircraft carriers were in reacting quickly to a military crisis. Long before any ground forces could reinforce the Republic of South Korea US Navy carrier aircraft were in action, and even after UN forces were mobilized in strength, the carriers continued to provide accurate ground support, while battleships and cruisers pounded shore targets.

The lesson of Korea was that navies were good for 'crisis-management' but no use once a major war had broken out. The four-minute warning of a nuclear exchange would not give sea power time to exert the slightest influence, so the argument ran, and it is interesting to note that this highly questionable theory still has a number of adherents today. What could not be questioned, however, was that navies were able to react more promptly and, what is more important, more flexibly to the long run of crises which have disturbed the peace of the world. Perhaps the best example is the Cuban Missile Crisis of 1963, when the Russians tried to set up missile bases in Cuba. The US Air Force could have bombed Cuba, and there is no doubt that the Army could have invaded the island, but both options ignored any risk of conflict with the Soviet Union. It was left to the US Navy to institute a 'blockade' through which Soviet merchant ships carrying missiles would not be allowed to pass. And so, while the world held its breath, the US Navy quietly turned back all the missile-carrying ships, without a shot being fired. Common sense and sea power had achieved something which mere military might could not.

Given that sea power has a part to play in today's

world, what forces are at work? The answer is that three factors more than any others have changed naval warfare: electronics, guided weapons and nuclear power. The revolution brought about by electronics is simply an acceleration of the process started when radar went to sea in the late 1930s. But, whereas the electron at sea was originally used to provide surveillance or early warning of attack, it is now at the heart of every form of naval activity. Electronics now provide the commander of a warship with information about when to fire his own weapons; they tell the engineer at what speed a propeller should be turning, and they even tell the shipyard what spares are needed.

Although primitive guided weapons were used in World War II the missile age did not start until the mid-1950s, when the US Navy converted two heavy cruisers into missile ships, arming them with surface-to-air missiles to defend the Fleet against attacks from Soviet bombers. As missiles became more effective the chances of a manned bomber penetrating a fleet's air defense became more remote. Not only could the bomber be hit before it got within bombing range, but

Top: The Belgian light frigate *Westhinder* is armed with Exocet missiles but her main function is as an antisubmarine escort.
Above: The 7000-ton Japanese destroyer *Hiei* has an unusual complement of three Sea King ASW helicopters.
Left: A Harpoon antiship missile is launched from the frigate USS *Knox*.

carrier aircraft could strike even further away, using their own air-to-air weapons to shoot down intruders. It was this ability to provide an outer layer of defense, 150 miles or more away from the Fleet, that gave the big aircraft carrier its preeminence in the 1960s and early 1970s.

The drawback to the carrier is its cost, which is in itself only a reflection of the phenomenal increase in the cost of weaponry. At current prices a nuclear carrier and her aircraft will cost $3.5 billion: each aircraft's cost is reckoned in tens of millions, and a typical air group of 80–90 aircraft will cost as much as the carrier itself. The benefits that a fleet gains from having such a ship with it are immense, both in offense and defense; the question is only, can such an expensive unit look after itself well enough to justify the expense, or could an equal degree of effectiveness be achieved in some other way?

The debate has been at times acrimonious, not least because the cost of maintaining big carriers became so enormous in the 1960s that several navies deliberately opted out of the race. Vulnerability to missiles and submarine torpedoes is the commonest criticism; but the question which the critics have not been able to answer is, what alternative form of warship could strike so hard and at the same time contribute so much to protect other ships? The real answer appears to be that the price of sea power has simply risen, and that a navy which wishes to control the oceans is going to have to pay for the privilege.

Weapons have become more expensive because they do more. When it became too dangerous for bombers to attack ships directly the logical solution was to develop 'stand-off' weapons, ie antiship guided missiles. The result is a continuing race between defense and attack, with designers matching developments and then being outmatched in turn. In the late 1960s antiship missiles were really pilotless aircraft, and as such offered no greater problem to ship defenses than a manned aircraft. To improve the missile's chances of getting through the designers then made it fly lower, and a new generation of 'sea-skimmers' came into being. Now the radar designers have produced radars which can detect a sea-skimmer, and the threat is receding.

The area in which electronics has made most

Left: The USS *Davidson* one of the *Garcia* class escorts which were built in the 1960s.
Right: The *Georges Leygues* is lead ship of a new class of large French antisubmarine destroyers. They are propelled by Rolls-Royce gas turbines and French-made diesels.
Main picture: Against all predictions the battleship *New Jersey* commissioned for the fourth time in 1983 and was soon deployed to the Mediterranean to join the units supporting the US peace-keeping forces in the Lebanon.
Bottom left: The Soviet Kashin class destroyers were the first large gas-turbine driven warships and have since been refitted with SS-N-2 antiship missiles.

D640
62

change is in the way in which information is handled. The power of the computer has been harnessed to handle the vast amount of information, process it so that it can be displayed, and then provide aids to the operator to assist him in making the right response. It has been called 'push-button' warfare but that is too simple a way to describe what has happened. The speed with which the computer can handle information allows the presentation of data in such a way that an operator can think about how to respond, whereas before he would be fully occupied in reacting to a mass of radar contacts, tactical instructions from the flagship, and possibly even sending instructions to other ships.

The application of electronics to all the functions of naval warfare has inevitably led to electronic warfare, the term for the struggle which goes on between rival operators to guess each other's intentions, purely by analyzing electronic activity. At its simplest it is jamming of hostile messages and radar transmissions, but it has been refined to take in analysis of signals and an elaborate bluff and double-bluff is the result. The basic rule of electronic warfare is that any weapon which relies on the transmission of electrical energy can ultimately be affected by the correct counter-application of electrical energy. Similarly any other form of sensor can be induced to 'see' or 'hear' something which is not there. The magic in electronic warfare lies in knowing exactly where the enemy's weak point lies.

The effect of electronics on weapons has been to give them precision, so much so that the ultimate goal of 'one round, one hit' comes close to being a reality. Therefore fewer rounds need to be fired, but of course the unit cost is astronomical, so very few can be afforded. In the Falklands air-sea battles only a couple of dozen surface-to-air missiles were fired by the ships, little more than the contents of the magazine

HMS *Mermaid* had a checkered career. Built originally for Ghana, but canceled incomplete after a coup, she was eventually bought and completed for the Royal Navy as a training frigate. She was transferred to the Malaysian Navy in 1977 and is now the *Hang Tuah*.

of one of the air-defense destroyers. Laser-guidance is now being applied even to shells, giving them a degree of precision never imagined before, but inevitably the cost rises considerably.

One side-effect of all this is to make the task of assessing fighting power much harder. A guided missile by itself is merely a complex package of instruments and wiring. Only when it functions as part of a 'weapon system' does it become effective in any way. The outward signs of such a system are unimpressive, maybe a rotating launcher and a tracker radar dish. The major part of the system lies below decks – the computers, processors and displays, not to mention cabling, cooling plant and the magazine. As the performance of radars and the capabilities of the data-handling system are kept secret, it is difficult to say at a glance how Ship A might differ in fighting power from Ship B. And yet, such is the importance of electronics that a ship without a good suite of electronics will be sunk by a well-equipped opponent before she even realizes that she is under attack.

The design of ships has also been transformed by the electronic revolution. Since the 1960s it has become the dominant influence on building-cost, to the extent that the hull now costs less than ten percent of the whole warship. Navies took some time to come to terms with the shift in emphasis, and there were several attempts to save money by cutting numbers of missiles, without realizing that the system has to be paid for, whether the ship carries 10 missiles or 100. Slowly the truth has emerged, that the design of cheap but effective warships is a very difficult and complex task. It is easy to design a warship which is neither seaworthy nor battleworthy, whereas compressing fighting power into a small platform tests the skill of the designers to the utmost.

One elementary way in which electronics affected

LEAHY

ship-design was the demand for technicians to maintain the equipment. Until integrated circuits became commonplace each ship had to accommodate numerous extra technicians. As they are generally better paid than sailors they contributed to the cost of running ships, and to tempt them to serve at sea there had to be an all-round increase in habitability. Today the wage bill takes up half the annual budget, and the cost of manning has led to extensive automation in gun mountings and engine rooms, to quote two examples. Improved habitability led to larger ships, and to an older generation of critics modern warships looked like luxury yachts rather than fighting ships. To an officer used to crowded warships of an earlier age it is not obvious that the greater size and volume of a modern warship has done little to push up its cost.

If a ship designed in the 1950s were to be redesigned for greater habitability today, she would cost very little more, and might be a better seaboat. She would, however, look very lightly armed by comparison, and there would be immediate pressure on the designers to pack in more weapons, and that would make her much more expensive. A modern warship's electronics

Left: Close up of the Top Sail surveillance radar of a Soviet Kresta II class cruiser.
Opposite: A stern view of the guided missile cruiser USS *Leahy* (CG.9) shows her after missile launcher and two radar trackers.
Below: The Japanese destroyer escort *Ishikara* on trials.

621

Top left: A French *Durance* class replenishment ship refuels the corvette *Aconit*.
Top right: The Soviet salvage ship *Aldan* which acts as an intelligence gatherer (AGI).
Above: HMS *Arrow*, a British Type 21 frigate.
Left: A Soviet radar picket ship, converted from a T.43 class minesweeper.

are comparatively light but need plenty of space for maintenance. The temptation to pack in more weapons to fill these 'empty' spaces has to be resisted by the designer, even if the ship appears to be big enough to accommodate them. The dispute between designers and naval staffs has become quite bitter in recent years, especially when Russian warships appear to bristle with weapons.

The vexed question of who has better ships, the West or the Soviet Union, is rarely understood, even by people in uniform. All too often there is no direct comparison of types: it is meaningless to compare a 9000-ton Soviet cruiser with a 3000-ton American frigate, but it is often done. Comparison is also hampered by the inclination of Western Intelligence to credit Soviet ships with extremely good performance. Every category of new Soviet warship is credited with ultra-high speed, and only after some years does the figure slide downwards. What is happening now is that the latest Soviet warships are showing signs of Western ideas on size and habitability, just as the hue and cry to increase the armament of Western warships reaches a crescendo.

Talk of Soviet warships and their imagined speeds leads us to the subject of marine propulsion. Paradoxically this is an area in which warship-design has been improved significantly, but at the same time speeds remain modest. There is no longer the search for speed, which pushed battleship-speeds from 23 to 28 knots between 1922 and 1937, nor the pursuit of 40-knot destroyers which was such a feature of the 1930s. Today's warships are mostly given modest speeds of 28–30 knots, sufficient to give tactical flexibility but not at the cost of fuel-consumption or reliability. This philosophy, common to NATO navies, was the outcome of World War II experience, but the rise in world oil prices since 1973 would have made it

F 92

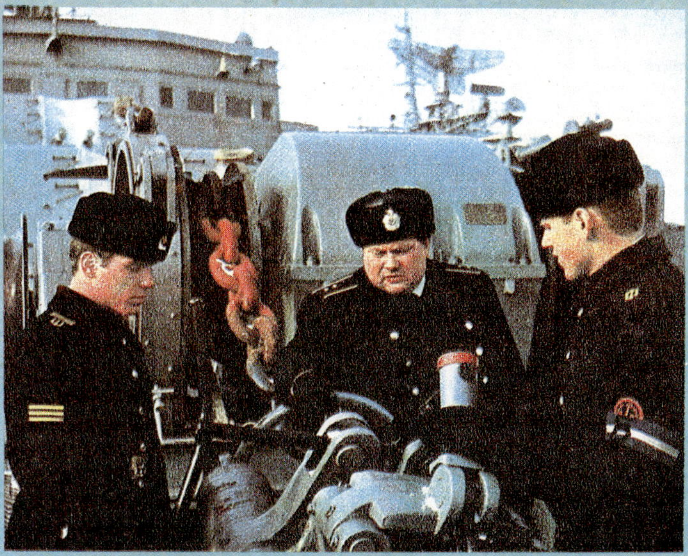

mandatory. A speed of 40 knots would not enable a ship to outrun a missile nor give her any greater ability to sink nuclear submarines, so a reasonable turn of speed which does not push up operating costs is good enough. If high-speed pursuit is needed the helicopter can do it faster and better.

The helicopter has transformed antisubmarine warfare, but at the cost of further complicating the design of warships. Space must be found for a hangar and flight deck, but the ship must also be a relatively stable platform in rough weather. A large square hangar acts as a wind trap and does nothing to help ship handling. Ideally a hangar should not be right aft, where the ship's rolling and pitching motion is at its worst, but siting it further forward impinges on weapons and radars. Another attribute of the helicopter is its ability to look over the horizon, a role which is becoming more and more important as the range of weapons increases.

Above left: An officer gives instruction in seamanship aboard a Soviet destroyer. The Soviet Navy relies on conscript sailors and is believed to suffer from maintenance problems because of their low standard of training.
Far left: HMS *Boxer*, the first of the 'Stretched' Type 22, frigates built for the Royal Navy. Following experience in the Falklands later ships of this class will have a 4.5-inch gun, double the outfit of missiles and two point defense gun systems.
Main picture: Soviet sailors relax on the fantail of a Riga class destroyer escort. Large numbers of these 1000-ton escorts were built in the 1950s.

The importance of navies in peacetime 'crisis-management' has been mentioned, but more than ever, there is a need for good communications. To Command, Control and Communications must be added Intelligence, hence the term C3I. A local commander must be in touch with his superiors, either in the flagship many miles away or even ashore 8000 miles away. Communications from ship-to-ship and ship-to-shore must be secure, ie they must not be intercepted or jammed by the enemy. Aircraft and ships must identify the target before firing a missile, a worry which is most acute in the 'Cold War', when a mistake could precipitate a major conflict. With missiles which can fly beyond horizon range this risk becomes acute; the Tomahawk cruise missile has a range of 300 miles, and as propellants and engines are improved the ranges of all missiles are likely to increase.

The submarine's impact on naval warfare is discussed in a later chapter, but it has had an overall effect on tactics that compares with that of the aircraft in World War II. Nuclear power created the 'true submarine', capable of running for weeks and months without coming to the surface to recharge batteries. It also gave the submarine speed, which it had not had before, so that now only the fastest ships can run away from it. At one time there was talk of the submarine taking over entirely from surface warships, but as always, the planners came up against the hard facts of sea power; if merchant ships have to cross the surface

Top left: A fine view showing the twin contra-rotating rotors of the Kamov Ka-25 Hormone-A, the standard Soviet shipboard antisubmarine helicopter.
Top right: The Anglo-French Lynx helicopter can operate a 'dunking' sonar, or as shown here, Sea Skua missiles.
Above: A Ka-25 hovers over her parent Kresta II class antisubmarine cruiser.
Right: Admiral of the Fleet of the Soviet Union and Deputy Minister of Defense Sergei Georgiyevich Gorshkov, father of the modern Soviet Navy.

of the sea, warships will have to protect them. The long search for ways of countering submarines is beginning to produce results, but it is fair to say that the problem has hindered the development of aggressive tactics by the Western Alliance.

The problem for the West is more acute than it is for the Soviet bloc. The West is an interlocking commercial and industrial grouping of nations, loosely bound by trade; it relies on free communication to maintain prosperity, and would therefore be even more reliant on communications in time of war. In a time of growing instability it has become apparent that free passage of raw materials and goods is just as vital to the wellbeing of Third World countries as it is to the developed nations.

The Soviet Union, as a huge land mass with an ample supply of raw materials, has no such problem, and can devote her energies to defending that land mass without the distraction of having to protect international trade. It is the classic dilemma of sea power versus land power – land power always holds the interior lines of communication, but sea power can choose weak points on the periphery. To do that it must, however, be able to guarantee the safe passage of raw materials by air and by sea. There should be no conflict between the need for control of the air and control of the oceans. Control of the former by itself will not secure the passage of *sufficient* raw materials or military supplies; control of the latter without control of the air is meaningless.

Top: The majority of Soviet intelligence gathering vessels are of the trawler type shown here, with good endurance and seakeeping qualities.
Center: The *Spruance* class destroyer USS *Elliott*.
Above: Despite 20 years of tests hovercraft are only now becoming accepted in military roles – as mine hunters or assault craft.
Right: A Hormone helicopter silhouetted against the setting sun.

The premier sea power is the United States, whose Navy has dominated the world since 1945. Its major partners are the North Atlantic Treaty Organization navies, which share in a common command structure for the defense of the Eastern Atlantic and the Mediterranean. The various European navies share the responsibility for defense of their own areas, and contribute forces to joint exercises, and of course from time to time international and local exercises are held. The US Navy, however, has widespread commitments outside NATO, and bases powerful fleets in the Mediterranean, the Atlantic and the Pacific.

The accession of Admiral Sergei Gorshkov to the post of Commander-in-Chief of the Soviet Navy in the mid-1950s is often claimed to be the start of Russian naval expansion, but Gorshkov has only given a modern form to a long-felt yearning for a major navy. We often forget that three previous attempts by the Russians to build a world-beating navy have only been stopped by major catastrophes, once by the Japanese,

a second time in 1914 and a third time in 1941. Gorshkov's predecessor, Kuznetsov, laid the foundations for a big navy after World War II, and many of the ships which appeared during the early Gorshkov years must have been planned before he took over.

The Soviet Fleet covers four oceans, of which the Northern Fleet and the Pacific Fleet are best placed to threaten Western sea lines of communication, mainly because they have free access to the open sea. The Baltic Fleet is not hemmed in during peacetime but NATO light forces would have little difficulty in blocking its exit route. Similarly the Black Sea Fleet has to negotiate the Dardanelles, and would find it almost impossible to force a way through such an easily defended strait. However, this could be circumvented by getting as many units as possible to sea at the start of a crisis.

Left: The advanced McDonnell Douglas F/A-18 Hornet is the US Navy's new interceptor and strike aircraft.
Bottom left: The Canadian destroyer escort *Nipigan* can operate a Sea King antisubmarine helicopter.
Below: HMS *Broadsword* was the first operational warship fitted with the Sea Wolf anti-missile system.

A major feature of Soviet naval strategy is a worldwide Ocean Surveillance System, which has as its aim the pinpointing of all major Western surface forces as well as submarines (wherever possible), to permit neutralization of such forces before they could attack the Soviet Union. To this end scores of intelligence-gathering ships trail Western task forces. In particular carrier groups are 'marked' to ensure that if hostilities broke out the carriers could be attacked by saturating waves of missiles fired from submarines, surface ships or aircraft.

The US Navy seemed to be powerless to offset this threat, with a fleet hit badly by block obsolescence, but the Russian challenge was finally met in the 1970s. The Reagan Administration in particular declared its intention of restoring a 600-ship navy, with 15 carrier battle groups, and is pouring vast sums into new programs to restore the balance. What must be worrying the Soviet Navy is that their policy of challenging American sea supremacy has merely alerted the enemy, at the moment that their big fleet built in the 1960s is approaching block obsolescence.

It is a common fallacy that totalitarian states like the Soviet Union have no limits on expenditure, and that naval expansion can be funded indefinitely. This is not true, and everything must sooner or later be paid for, in one currency or another. Resources made available to the Soviet Navy are resources which cannot be applied elsewhere. It remains to be seen whether inter-service rivalry will hamper future expansion of the Soviet Navy, which has been receiving the lion's share of funding in recent years.

Many Western defense commentators have identified 1984–85 as a crucial point in this process. Admiral Gorshkov must retire, and it is hard to see that a man of similar stature, with his personal political support at the highest level, will succeed him. There will also be the problem of finding money to pay for a new generation of warships capable of matching the latest American technology. The Air Forces and the Strategic Rocket Forces in particular will be using the opportunity to reassert their claims to preferential treatment, and the military budget will almost certainly be hard to balance.

Lest this should sound gratifying to Western ears, it should be remembered that the last time such a state of affairs existed was 1914, when the attempt by Admiral Tirpitz to challenge British sea power created the tension which led to World War I. A military hierarchy in dire financial straits can be tempted to look at war as a way out of its difficulties . . .

2. STRATEGIC WEAPONS

HMS *Revenge*, one of the four British Polaris nuclear-powered ballistic missile submarines. Built in the late 1960s, they will be replaced by four Trident boats in the late 1980s.

Until the 1950s navies were undoubtedly outranked by armies and in particular air forces, because not even the United States Navy could boast of a long range ballistic missile. All that changed when in 1956 the US Navy was given permission to develop a solid-fuel intermediate range ballistic missile (IRBM), code-named Polaris.

The technical problems were formidable. Not only must the missile travel accurately along a ballistic trajectory to a target a thousand miles away, it must also be fired underwater and rise from the water before the main rocket motor ignites. Given that a whole range of new technologies had to be developed, the period of four years from the 1956 decision to the moment on 20 July 1960 when the submarine *George Washington* fired two operational UGM-27A Polaris A1s was remarkably short. By comparison the Soviets were able to deploy the SS-N-4 Sark IRBM in the *Golf* and *Hotel* class submarines by roughly the same time (1960–61) although the Sark had a range of only 300 miles and could not be launched underwater. Even the substitution of the SS-N-5 Serb missile, with a range of 700 miles only marginally increased their chance of surviving Western antisubmarine measures, and by 1967 the United States had moved on to the Polaris A3, with a range of 2880 miles.

The original Polaris and its nuclear-propelled submarine delivery platforms were virtually immune to a preemptive strike, primarily because Soviet antisubmarine forces could not operate in the areas in which the American, British and French nuclear ballistic submarines (SSBNs) would launch their missiles. So sure was the US Navy in its assurance of the SSBN's invulnerability that the successor to Polaris, the UGM-73A Poseidon was given the same range, and merely used its increased size to double the payload and provide greater accuracy and penetration aids ('penaids') to beat Soviet defenses.

All this changed when the Soviets developed the SS-N-8. When it was first deployed in 1973 Western Intelligence was deeply worried to learn that it had a range of 4800 miles, as against 2880 miles for Polaris A3 and Poseidon. It was also credited with a circular error probable (CEP) of about 1300ft, similar to the American land-based Minuteman. Unlike the Sark and Serb the SS-N-8 could be launched underwater, and the Delta type submarines had a configuration similar to Western SSBNs, for the first time. To add to Western fears, the SS-N-8 proved that it could outrange the successor to Poseidon, the as yet untried Trident; whereas Trident I was planned to have a range of 4350 miles the SS-N-8 showed that it could reach out to 5700 miles – making it a submarine-launched ICBM rather than an IRBM.

As Polaris had been originally conceived as a survivable system, which could retaliate if US land-based strategic forces were by some mischance to be destroyed, this Soviet development was unwelcome

news. US strategic planners had previously assumed that any Soviet 'first strike' would be on a massive scale, so that the Polaris submarines would have to launch their 'second strike' promptly. All that was needed to ensure the 'survivability' of Polaris was the issue of the necessary commands to the SSBNs at sea to fire. However, by the late 1960s it was becoming clear that a much bigger risk was the 'escalating' conventional war which culminates in a nuclear exchange – possibly even a limited one such as Sir John Hackett envisages in his book *The Third World War*, with Minsk and Birmingham (UK) wiped out but no other nuclear weapons used.

If such a sequence of events happens (and many believe that it fits more closely with Soviet thinking than the original idea of an immediate all-out exchange) a high-priority target for Soviet missiles would be US submarine bases and the Polaris, Poseidon and Trident command and control centers. As all the available SSBNs would have been sent to sea (including those already on station) they would now be running short of food and water, and equipment would be needing maintenance. They would also have been attacked by Soviet antisubmarine forces, and it must be assumed that some would have been located and destroyed – perhaps as many as half their number might be sunk or out of action.

Above: The USS *Ethan Allen* (SSBN.608), an early Polaris boat, is still in service carrying Poseidon missiles.
Below left: Soviet Yankee class submarines carry 16 SS-N-6 missiles.

Since the mid-1960s the Soviet Navy has undergone a subtle change in its makeup. As the strategic threat posed by the attack carriers' twin-engined bombers began to recede (or at least to appear less dangerous) the threat to the Russian heartland from Polaris missiles became more believable. And yet, how could the Polaris submarine be attacked, when they were operating in Western-dominated waters?

The answer was to push antisubmarine warfare (ASW) forces further out into those traditional 'friendly' seas, where they could quite legitimately track and identify Western submarines, so that on the outbreak of war they could be quickly attacked and sunk. Evidence for this change in tactics lies in the building of large numbers of powerful antisubmarine ships, culminating in the helicopter carriers *Leningrad* and *Moskva* and the hybrid cruiser carriers *Kiev* and *Minsk*. Even the development of weapons and tactics clearly intended to attack the US Navy's aircraft carriers reinforces the argument, for the Soviets know that the 'sanctuary' provided by carrier air power in the Mediterranean, for example, prevents their ASW forces from tracking SSBNs.

128
726

Main picture: The USS *Ohio* (SSBN.726), first of the giant Trident submarines which each carry 24 missiles so that the same level of deterrence can be maintained with fewer hulls (earlier US ballistic missile submarines carry 16 missiles each).
Top left: Loading the canister containing a Trident I missile aboard the *Ohio*.
Below: The commanding officer of the *Ulysses S. Grant* (SSBN.631) standing at the periscope.

One of the most powerful arguments, therefore, for developing a longer-ranged Submarine-Launched Ballistic Missile (SLBM) is the need to get the SSBNs further away from hostile ASW forces – for the Americans this means closer to the Atlantic and Pacific seaboards, and for the Russians it means the Arctic and the Black Sea, where friendly aircraft and ships can provide cover. In other words, the SSBN becomes no more than a mobile vehicle for getting the SLBMs out of harbor and beneath the waves.

There were other unrelated reasons for the US Navy to reorganize its SSBN fleet of 41 Polaris and Poseidon submarines, the need to streamline maintenance and to enable each SSBN to spend a greater proportion of its service life 'on station'. This feature, combined with the Undersea Long-range Missile System (ULMS) proposed in 1967, promised a more efficient and cost effective underwater deterrent for the 1980s and 1990s, but it was not until the end of 1972 that Lockheed received the development contract for the C4 Trident. Initial plans were to retrofit 10 (later 12) of the *Lafayette* and *Benjamin Franklin* classes of SSBN with 16 Trident missiles, and to replace the remaining 31 SSBNs with 16 new *Ohio* class, carrying 24 Tridents each.

With a submerged displacement of 18,700 tons the *Ohio*'s were the largest submarines ever designed, although subsequently eclipsed in size by the Soviet *Typhoon* type (30,000 tons). Apart from their massive length of 560ft overall they are similar to the earlier SSBNs, with the Trident missiles launched from a double row of vertical tubes abaft the sail. Although SSBNs are not intended to take offensive action against surface ships or other submarines, for self-defense they are armed with four 21-inch torpedo tubes, angled out to port and starboard, ahead of the sail, and they have a big BQQ-6 spherical sonar in the bow compartment.

The first of the US Navy's Trident submarines, the USS *Ohio* (SSBN-726) went to sea at the end of 1981, and her sisters *Michigan*, *Florida*, *Georgia*, *Rhode Island* and *Alabama* are in varying stages of construction. Another ten, numbered SSBN.732-741 are authorized, and the cost of the latest is running at more than $350 million. Backing them up are ten earlier SSBNs, converted from Poseidon to Trident in 1978–82, starting with the *Francis Scott Key* and ending with the *Casimir Pulaski* in 1982. Ten older boats, the *Ethan Allen* and *George Washington* classes were reclassified as attack submarines (SSNs) in 1980, which involved cutting them into three sections, removing the 16 missile tubes and then re-welding the forward and after sections together. This elaborate procedure was necessary to comply with the terms of the first Strategic Arms Limitation Treaty (SALT 1), which limited the number of nuclear warheads each side could deploy.

The Soviet Delta class of SSBNs falls into three distinct categories. The Delta I (bottom) carries 12 SS-N-8 missiles with over 5000 miles range. Delta II (center) increased the number of SS-N-8 missiles to 16 but the Delta III (top) has the much larger SS-N-18 missile which can carry up to seven warheads. The extra height of this missile accounts for the more prominent 'hump' abaft the sail.

The Soviet equivalent to the American SSBNs was the 9300-ton Yankee class, which, unlike the earlier boats, had SS-N-6 missiles with a range of 1100–1600 miles. In all 34 of these submarines were built before production switched to the 10,000-ton Delta I, which had 12 tubes carrying the long range SS-N-8. After 18 were built a slightly larger type, the 11,400-ton Delta II, was built, with 16 missiles. In 1979 the Delta III appeared, its higher casing over the missile tubes indicating a longer missile; this was codenamed SS-N-18 by NATO, and it is believed to be a 4000-mile range missile with no fewer than seven warheads in one version.

The impact of the SS-N-8 on Western planning has already been mentioned, but this was nothing compared to the psychological shock when in 1981 the Pentagon revealed the existence of the *Typhoon* class, displacing 30,000 tons and 600ft long, and armed with a missile tentatively identified as SS-NX-20 (the 'X' signifying experimental). It was no use commentators pointing out that SSBNs are not intended to fight one another, and that sheer size is not a measure of fighting power (almost certainly the greater size of Soviet missiles is largely a reflection of their designers' inability to design smaller rocket motors). As far as public opinion was concerned, the Soviets had outflanked the West.

The reality was that American technology was still ahead, and that the cruise missile would more than redress the balance in strategic forces. As we have seen, the main aim of the Russian naval effort is directed towards tracking the big American carriers and their battle groups. To achieve that objective the Soviets have carefully built up an elaborate worldwide surveillance system, using ships' radars, submarines' sonars, maritime patrol aircraft and reconnaissance satellites to provide hour-by-hour information on the whereabouts of US Navy and NATO surface units. Known as the Soviet Ocean Surveillance System (SOSS), it is operated by 'snoopers' of all kinds, even down to radar-equipped trawlers known as AGIs, which appear with monotonous regularity whenever Western warships carry out exercises. Although at first sight SOSS seems foolproof it has the basic weakness of being vulnerable to saturation and deception; if too much information is fed into SOSS the Soviets have to guess where the real threat is located.

The cruise missile lends itself to such deception, for it is in reality only a weapon-carrying pilotless aircraft, which can fly long distances on preprogrammed flight paths, using electronic 'maps' stored

Above: The 6000-ton attack submarine USS *Phoenix*, being launched, is dwarfed by the first two Trident boats *Ohio* and *Michigan*.
Left: 'Sherwood Forest' – the massive missile tubes on the lower deck of the *Ohio*.
Opposite: The French SSBN *l'Indomptable* under construction at Cherbourg. Construction of deep-diving nuclear submarines requires special steel and heavy shielding for the reactor.

in its computer memory. It can be fired from the deck of a warship or from the torpedo tubes of a submarine, and so can form part of a 'mix' of other weapons. Its warhead can be high explosive or nuclear, and its payload can even be used to put airfields out of action.

The question of whether a Tomahawk cruise missile (the naval variant) is better at penetrating Soviet defenses becomes irrelevant, for the deployment of a comparatively small number of missiles among all the other anti-submarine, antiaircraft and antiship weapons already at sea in Western warships would complicate Russian problems immensely. SOSS would have to track every NATO warship which could *in theory* be armed with strategic cruise missiles. In the words of one distinguished commentator, a few sea-based strategic cruise missiles seem a low price to pay for what may be a major dilution of SOSS effectiveness. It poses to the Russians the same sort of Hydra-headed threat that the SS-20 poses to NATO's land forces.

Current plans are to launch Tomahawk from torpedo tubes, in the same way as Sub-Harpoon and Subroc missiles are, an option which limits the number of rounds which can be carried. Another solution is to insert vertical launching tubes at either end of the pressure hull of attack submarines. Two basic variants of Tomahawk have been designed, a tactical type with a range of some 300nm (nautical miles) and a strategic type with a range of 1500nm. The tactical variant has a conventional blast warhead based on that of the Bullpup-B, while the strategic variant carries a weight of nuclear explosive equal in weight to 1000 pounds of high explosive.

Although the cruise missile has been termed the 'Doomsday Doodlebug' it is nothing new. The German V-1 of 1944–45 was a land-launched cruise missile, while in the 1950s US submarines were armed with the air-breathing Regulus I and Regulus II nuclear cruise missiles. What has changed is the technology; the Tomahawk uses inertial guidance and a terrain-matching radar known as TERCOM to fly at low level and to keep it on course. All that is needed to make the system effective is the provision of accurate radar-altitude maps of potential target areas. Unfortunately for the United States and its allies considerable opposition to cruise missiles has been whipped up, and President Carter seemed willing to consider a three-year protocol to the Salt II Treaty (negotiated but still unsigned), under which cruise missiles with a range of more than 375 miles would have been banned for three years.

No such inhibitions were attached to the 'stretched' version of Trident, the D5 Trident II. The need for a longer range had been foreseen, but the need to be able to update the Poseidon-armed SSBNs had forced designers to design the first ULMS with a 72-inch body which could fit into Poseidon tubes. The *Ohio* class submarines could be built with larger-diameter (82inch) tubes, which were then given liners to take the Trident I until such time as Trident II was ready. Trident I (UGM-93A) now weighs 70,000 pounds and can carry up to 24 multiple independently targeted reentry vehicles (MIRVs); the D5 Trident II will have a range of 6000 miles, but it is still under development, and will not come into service until 1986 or 1987.

The introduction of the *Ohio* class SSBNs is

bedeviled by the rapidity with which the original Polaris program was implemented; block obsolesence means that the first SSBNs reached the end of their useful life in 1980, and even the later *Lafayette* and *Benjamin Franklin* classes, whose hull-lives are five years longer, will have to be scrapped by the later 1980s and early 1990s. Putting 24 Tridents into each *Ohio* was just a way of avoiding the staggering cost of replacing all 41 SSBNs (in Fiscal Year 1981 the cost for one *Ohio* was $1.5 billion).

The biggest drawback to the submarine-based nuclear deterrent is the difficulty of communicating with a submerged submarine. The US Navy's current Very Low Frequency (VLF) radio can penetrate water to a very limited degree, and that means that SSBNs must come close to the surface at prearranged times to receive messages. Transmitting causes fewer problems, as security demands that SSBNs should not broadcast except in the gravest emergency. At present the US Navy maintains a force of 12 EC-130 TACAMO (TAke Command And Move Out) aircraft to provide an airborne link. The next development may be an Extra Low Frequency (ELF) system which can transmit through the earth's crust, and after that blue-green lasers may provide the answer, but that technology is not likely to be around until the next century.

As the *Ohio* class come into commission they are sent to a new base at Bangor, Washington if assigned to the Pacific Fleet, where they join the remaining 10 Polaris boats. Atlantic Fleet submarines are currently forward-based at Holy Loch on the Firth of Clyde in Scotland (the Pacific counterpart is Guam), but the Trident boats will be based at King's Bay in Georgia. The reason for this redisposition is not simply because of the additional range of Trident but to provide a new level of support and maintenance.

European fears of being abandoned to Soviet aggression led to the creation of parallel nuclear forces by France and the United Kingdom. Until 1963 the British relied solely on air-launched nuclear weapons,

HMS *Resolution* in the Gareloch, home base of the British Polaris submarine force.

Right: The commanding officer of the British SSBN *Repulse* at the periscope. Modern periscopes have such refinements as thermal imagers, film cameras and laser rangefinders.
Far right: Artist's impression of the massive new Soviet Typhoon class which differs from all previous SSBNs in having the missile compartment ahead of the sail.
Below: A Sea King helicopter winches a crewman off the after casing of the British SSBN HMS *Resolution*.

but their hopes of buying a replacement for their Vulcan bomber were dashed when the US Air Force canceled the Skybolt air-launched ballistic missile. Instead the British were offered Polaris, and the momentous decision was made to build five (later cut to four) SSBNs for the Royal Navy. The hull and reactor was to be British in design, but the missile compartment and fire control system were provided by the US Navy.

The keel of the first SSBN, HMS *Resolution* was laid early in 1964, and she went to sea in October 1967. The last, HMS *Revenge* was laid down only 15 months later, and went to sea at the end of 1969. It was a remarkable achievement, for the first British nuclear submarine, HMS *Dreadnought* had only been commissioned ten months before the *Resolution* was laid down, and yet the entire project was on time and within budget.

The British SSBN force is based at the Gareloch, not far from the American SSBNs at Holy Loch. Many observers have commented on the vulnerability of both bases to mining, but in fact they were deliberately chosen because they are hard to block. Although called 'sea lochs', they are similar to Norwegian fjords in having very deep water, so deep that in an emergency an SSBN could leave harbor submerged. In peacetime a tug accompanies each SSBN as she leaves, to reduce any risk of collision with merchant shipping in the Clyde, but this is to provide public reassurance. Another important reason for basing SSBNs on the Clyde is the high noise-level from shipping, which makes it very hard for Russian submarines to maintain a listening watch.

As the most forward Polaris bases, Holy Loch and the Gareloch are kept under constant surveillance by the Soviet Navy, who are believed to keep a submarine on a 24-hour watch in the Clyde Approaches. For some years this has been countered by keeping a sonar-equipped guard ship in the area, tracking 'Ivan' and giving British and American submarines timely warning of his movements. The British have permanent base facilities at HMS *Neptune* but the Americans use a submarine tender moored in Holy Loch.

The biggest difficulty encountered by the British strategic deterrent force is caused by the cancellation of the fifth submarine. In 1964 the incoming Labour Government was forced to retreat from its pledge to scrap the Polaris submarines, but the new Defence Minister Denis Healey made a gesture of appeasement to the party's left wing by canceling the fifth submarine. This ill-judged economy puts a heavy strain on the men who man the submarines and the civilians who have to maintain them. To maintain the nuclear deterrent it is essential that one submarine is always at sea, and although this has caused great difficulties at times, the SSBN force has always remained operational. Like the US Navy's Blue and Gold manning system, the Royal Navy operates Port and Starboard crews, who do a rapid exchange at the end of each mission and immediately take the submarine back to sea for another three month patrol.

Life on board Polaris submarines is not particularly arduous, apart from the strain of maintaining strict radio silence and not surfacing for three months. The biggest problems are to keep fit and mentally alert while living in comparatively cramped quarters, with no sunshine. Boredom is the great enemy, and every effort is made to keep officers and men occupied. Apart from the high rates of pay, the biggest inducement is the long leave and the ability to plan time with families according to a predictable cycle of time at sea.

It had been hoped that France and Great Britain could share responsibility for a joint European submarine deterrent but a rift between France and the

United States exacerbated Anglo-French suspicion. It was said at the time that discussions between the Royal Navy and the *Marine Nationale* had only reached the subject of what to eat for breakfast before breaking down irrevocably. But for the French there was to be no purchase of American missiles, for the United States refused to sell the Polaris system to France.

Determined to achieve her goal of self-sufficiency in defense France went ahead with the development of her own SLBM, the Mer-Sol Ballistique Systeme (MSBS or Sea-to-Surface Ballistic System). The M-1 version of the missile was installed for trials in the experimental submarine *Gymnote* and then became operational in the SSBN *le Redoutable* in 1971. The next development, the 1300-mile M-2, went to sea in the third SSBN *le Foudroyant* in 1976 and was retro-fitted to the *Redoutable* and her sister *le Terrible*. The M-2 missile was followed by the M-20, and from 1987 *le Tonnant*, *l'Indomptable* and the earlier boats will receive the M-4.

A sixth SSBN of enlarged design, *l'Inflexible* was authorized in 1978, followed by a second unnamed unit a year later. The reason is officially that a constant patrol cannot be maintained with only five *Redoutable* class, but the more likely reason is simply the need to replace the first of that class, which will have been in commission for 20 years in 1991; by the end of the century even the others will be 20–27 years old. The M-4 missile will be a great improvement over the earlier missiles, having a range of 2500–3000 miles and six 150-kiloton MIRV warheads, but these improvements will not match even Trident I's performance.

For the British the problem of updating their deterrent was more acute, for unlike the French they had not had control over the development of their own SLBMs. Nor had they taken the opportunity to replace the A3 Polaris with Poseidon, and as all four *Resolution* class SSBNs were completed in 1967–69 they would become obsolete by the end of the 1980s. In the late 1970s a program codenamed Chevaline was initiated to update the A3 Polaris warhead by giving it

a partial MIRV capability, but in 1980 the Government announced that it would buy Trident I missiles and build a new class of SSBNs for them. However, this time the entire cost was to be put on the naval budget, whereas the cost of Polaris had been spread over the whole defense budget.

The need to find £1000 million out of the Royal Navy's slender budget from 1985 to 1995 provoked a furious discussion but even though the more expensive D5 Trident II is to be bought and the cost is therefore to be even greater than first thought, at the time of writing the Royal Navy still plans to build four *Vanguard* class Trident SSBNs. There has been discussion inside the Royal Navy about buying Tomahawk missiles instead and using them to arm the nuclear hunter-killer submarines, but the Government remains firmly committed to Trident, while the Labour Party, as before, has pledged itself to cancel the program.

The only other country to possess nuclear ballistic missile submarines is the People's Republic of China, but until recently progress has been slow as China's resources have been dedicated to other more urgent projects. In 1964 a single diesel-electric ballistic missile-firing submarine similar to the Soviet Golf class was completed at Luda in Manchuria. No sisters followed, and it was assumed by Western commentators that she was merely an experimental prototype. In August 1981 reports reached the West that a submarine of this type was sunk when a ballistic missile exploded on board, which suggests a setback to the program, but the year before the launch of an SSBN was reported. Although earlier land-based missiles were liquid-fueled the Chinese seem to have overcome any technical problems in making solid rocket fuel, the only obstacle to developing some sort of equivalent to the Western and Soviet SSBNs and their missiles.

It has always been assumed that the role of the SSBN would terminate on the outbreak of war, as her function was thought to be limited to 'second strike'. However as we have seen, they could easily find themselves in a protracted naval war, in which they would still play an important role. Like the King in a chess game they would have to be kept out of trouble and would be able to do little to win the war, but would be an absolutely crucial element in deciding the outcome. It is this paradox that leads some commentators to treat SSBNs as somehow different from 'normal' fighting ships, but they are just as much a part of modern naval warfare as any other type of warship.

SSBNs do not operate together but on one occasion it proved possible to photograph France's first three SSBNs *Redoutable, Terrible* and *Foudroyant* off Brest.

The *City of Corpus Christi* (SSN.705), one of the US Navy's *Los Angeles* class attack submarines. They are being built in large numbers as the standard SSN for the 1990s.

3. UNDERWATER WARFARE

More than any other single warship-type, the submarine has transformed naval warfare in recent years. The dream that had eluded designers in two world wars, the creation of a 'true submarine' independent of atmospheric oxygen, came to fruition in 1955. In January the USS *Nautilus* signaled 'underway on nuclear power', signifying that she could now travel submerged without having to use her snorkel to recharge batteries. While it was true that her crewmen still needed to eat and breathe, and that these two needs imposed some finite limit on the time that the *Nautilus* could spend submerged, she was no longer *forced* to come up for air at intervals, and therefore had much greater tactical freedom than ever before. With the steam generated by her nuclear heat-exchanger the *Nautilus* could also run for long periods at maximum power, down below the turbulence of wind and waves.

Within the year the US Navy had ordered more nuclear 'hunter-killer' or attack submarines, and by 1959 it was confirmed that no more 'conventional' diesel-electric submarines would be built for the US Navy. This was as much a reflection of the enormous cost of nuclear submarines (SSNs) as their outstanding qualities. Not only does each reactor demand a large capital investment but each submarine requires more highly trained engineers and technicians than a conventional 'boat' or SSK (hunter-killer submarine).

Under Stalin the Soviet Navy had built very large numbers of conventional submarines in the 1950s, nearly 300 of the Whiskey and Zulu classes. The intention was apparently to exploit captured German expertise, but all plans were thrown back in the melting pot with the advent of nuclear propulsion, and by the end of 1959 the first Russian-built SSN, a 4500-ton boat dubbed the November type by NATO, was at sea. By 1965 the total built was 14, and production had switched to the more successful Victor I and Victor II types.

As we saw in the previous chapter the logical follow-on from nuclear submarine propulsion was the submarine launched ballistic missile and the SSBN was the result. But there remained a need for the nuclear attack submarine, or SSN. She offered the only realistic countermeasure against the SSBN, for she could outrun the clumsier and heavier SSBN; she could also screen surface forces against attack, or take the offensive against enemy forces.

The SSN resembles earlier submarines in layout, with accommodation forward and propulsion aft, but because the ideal hull form for high underwater speed and maneuverability demands a single large propeller aft, the traditional after torpedo tubes have disappeared, and modern SSNs have only bow tubes. The latest US Navy submarines have a big spherical sonar in the bow compartment, and so the torpedo tubes have been moved further aft, angled outwards.

The standard weapon is still the torpedo, but sup-

plemented by longer range guided missiles for surface attack. The US Navy uses primarily the Mk 48 torpedo, which employs a sophisticated guidance system to 'home' itself onto a target, just like a guided missile. However, it differs in one important respect from atmospheric missiles: guidance is by means of a thin wire trailed out from a spool inside the torpedo. Two-way signals are passed down this wire, from the submarine's sonar to the torpedo's guidance system, and back from sensors in the torpedo's homing head to the main fire control system.

The reason for such complexity is that water is a comparatively opaque medium. Sound travels great distances underwater but it is very easily distorted by layers of differing temperature (called thermal layers), and even of differing salinity. Water is even more opaque to radio waves, so a submerged submarine is not able to communicate freely with other submarines or friendly surface warships. Surface warships enjoy the benefits of radio, radar and even visual signaling, but the submarine has to come to periscope depth to put up an aerial or from a slightly greater depth can unwind a trailing aerial before she can transmit. Extra low frequency messages can reach her from a shore station, but again the submarine must be close to the surface and the message will take a long time to get through.

The wire used for guiding torpedoes is similar to piano wire, and as it is light it hangs in the water, rather than sinking. There is a risk that if the submarine continues to close with her target she may overrun her own wire, and that it might entangle itself around the propeller, or that she might cut the wire. The reason why such an eventuality is not taken too seriously is that the engagement time is quite short; the torpedo may be traveling at a speed of 50 knots for 20,000 yards, which means that it will take only 12 minutes to reach maximum range. If the torpedo has failed to detonate the empty wire spool in the torpedo tube is ejected, and if the guidance wire is cut the

Left: The Soviet Echo I and II classes (an Echo II is shown) were originally armed with SS-N-3 Shaddock cruise missiles but several have been converted to SSNs.
Above left: No Soviet submarine has caused quite as much alarm in Western naval circles as the Alfa with its reputed 45 knots underwater speed and titanium hull permitting a diving depth of 3000 feet.
Below: A Soviet Foxtrot class diesel/electric submarine being shadowed in the Mediterranean by a US destroyer. At least 60 Foxtrots have been built in the USSR and a number have been exported.

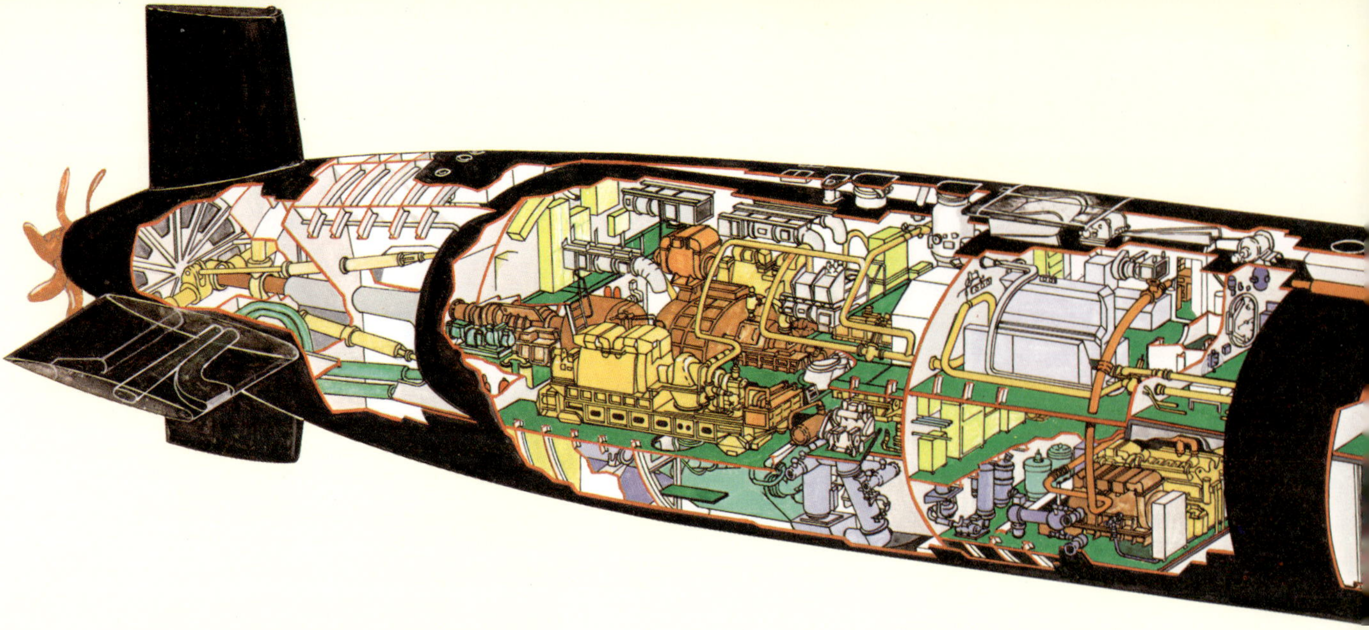

torpedo's own control system automatically switches to an 'autonomous' mode, in which it functions like an ordinary homing weapon. As the torpedo has its own active or passive acoustic sensor in its homing head, it can be used to send back information to the main fire control computer, and this means that in poor sonar conditions the torpedo itself can provide information about the target. One tactic is to use two torpedoes, one running at full speed and the other quietly on a separate track; if the target submarine hears the noise of the first torpedo's propellers he may turn in the direction of the second torpedo, without being aware of its nearness.

The virtue of the wire-guided torpedo is that it remains under positive control throughout its run, and so it cannot be jammed. However there are still a number of free-running torpedoes. In the war between Great Britain and Argentina in 1982 the nuclear submarine *Conqueror* used a pair of Mark 8 unguided compressed air torpedoes to sink the Argentinian cruiser *General Belgrano*, in spite of carrying a number of electrically driven wire-guided Tigerfish torpedoes. The reason is that the Tigerfish Mod O, being designed to attack deep-running submarines, is not good at tracking targets on the surface. The Mod 1 anti-ship weapon had not been fitted.

The sinking of the *General Belgrano* also showed how difficult it can be to communicate with modern submarines. On 2 May 1982 the cruiser and her two missile-armed destroyers were in position 55° 27′ South, 61° 25′ West. HMS *Conqueror* had been following her for some time, shadowing but prohibited from attacking under the 'rules of engagement' given to her captain. To the *Conqueror* there was the practical difficulty that if the three Argentine warships maintained their course they would cross the Burdwood Bank, whose maximum depth of 24 fathoms (144 feet) was far less than the minimum depth at which it is advisable for a large nuclear submarine to run at speed, especially when the submarine has no wish to reveal her presence by coming too close to the surface.

The Operations Staff back in Northwood, outside London, 8000 miles away, knew of the problem for the submarine, and also knew that the course of the Argentine surface action group was taking it close to British surface forces.

In spite of both submarine and surface forces being aware of the broad tactical situation, the Commander-in-Chief Fleet had to wait until a prearranged time when HMS *Conqueror* discreetly put up an aerial to receive any urgent messages. The import of the signal was clear; the rules of engagement were to be amended immediately to allow hostile warships in the vicinity of the *Conqueror* to be sunk. Shortly afterwards two Mark 8 torpedoes ripped into the cruiser, one blowing off her bow and the other crippling her rudders and propellers. From a military point of view the attack was fully justified, for if the information had been withheld from the submarine she would either have put herself in grave risk of damage or even destruction by crossing the Burdwood Bank or she would have had to break off the pursuit,

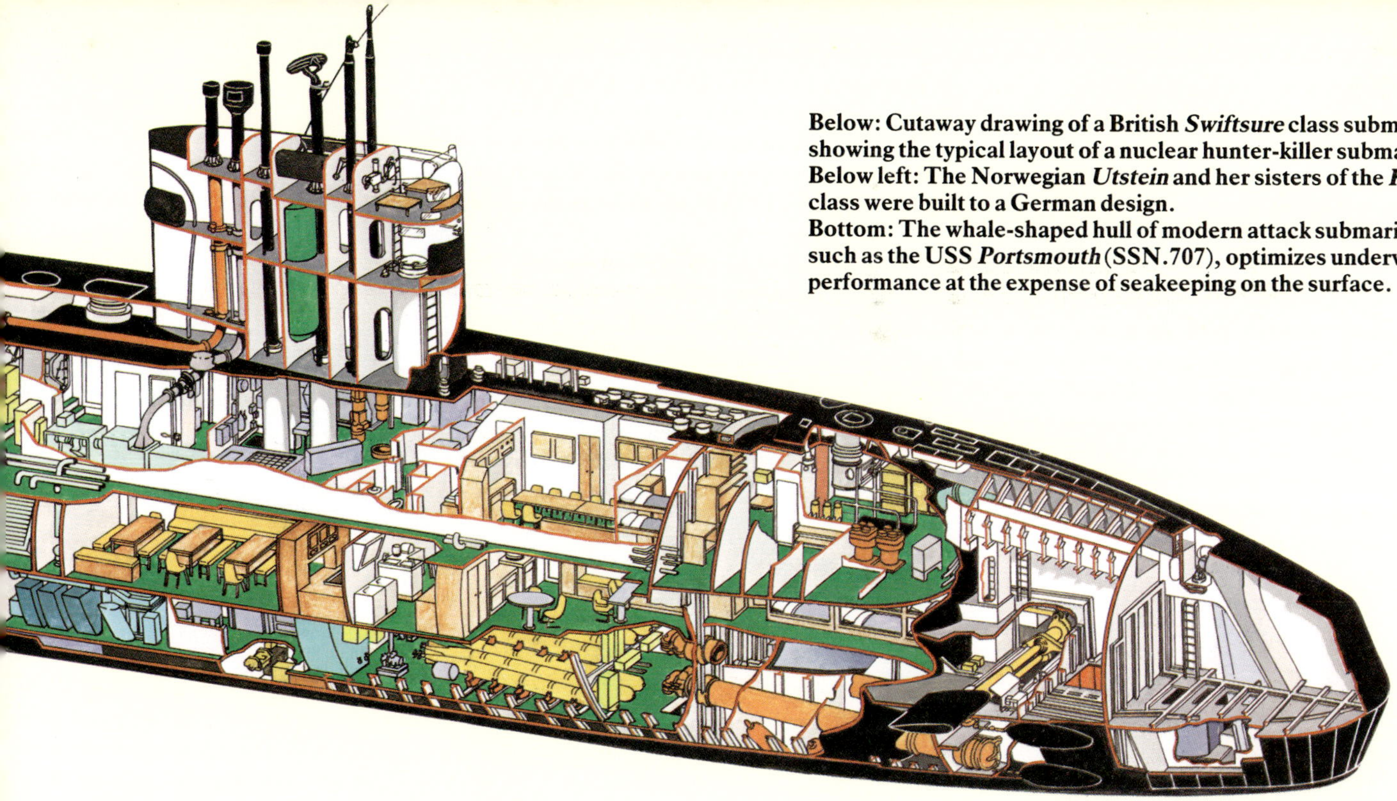

Below: Cutaway drawing of a British *Swiftsure* class submarine, showing the typical layout of a nuclear hunter-killer submarine.
Below left: The Norwegian *Utstein* and her sisters of the *Kobben* class were built to a German design.
Bottom: The whale-shaped hull of modern attack submarines, such as the USS *Portsmouth* (SSN.707), optimizes underwater performance at the expense of seakeeping on the surface.

leaving a powerful force equipped with Exocet missiles to get closer to the surface forces she was trying to protect.

Supplementing the torpedo rather than replacing it, is the submarine-launched antiship missile. The United States has developed a version of the Harpoon, designated UGM-84, capable of being launched from a torpedo tube. The missile is packed in a canister resembling a torpedo; when the canister is fired from the tube it rises to the surface slowly, being set at the correct angle by small actuating fins. As soon as the tip of the canister 'broaches' or breaks the surface of the water the cap blows off and the missile fires itself out of the canister as it would in the ordinary way. Target data, particularly the bearing relative to the submarine, have already been entered in the missile's computer, so that it can fly the intervening 60 miles on inertial guidance. Only when it is within the lethal radius of its target does the missile turn on its radar seeker, and it then enters its terminal or homing phase.

The French SM-39 version of the Exocet missile is similar, but with a shorter range. It has only recently become operational in the *Agosta* class diesel-electric submarines, and will equip the *Rubis* class SSNs.

The Soviet Navy produced its first Charlie class submarine in 1968, and Western intelligence sources were startled to note eight horizontal hatches on the forward casing. They turned out to contain a 30-mile range antiship missile designated the SS-N-7, and since then more Charlie IIs and the bigger Papa class have been built.

The US Navy is introducing an antiship variant of the Tomahawk cruise missile, with a range of 350 miles. The method of launching is exactly the same as that for Sub-Harpoon.

The practical problem of deploying such long range missiles is the difficulty of providing midcourse guidance. Without an aircraft, helicopter or warship closer to the target, the submarine launching a Tomahawk missile 200 miles away will have very little idea of the target's course and speed. There is another drawback; even the largest submarines have a limited amount of space in which reload missiles and torpedoes can be stowed. The mission of each submarine will therefore have to be closely examined, to decide how many of each type must be embarked.

Very few countries can afford the luxury of nuclear submarines. The Royal Navy started work on its prototype, HMS *Dreadnought* in 1959, using an American Westinghouse S5W reactor similar to those in the US *Skipjack* class. She commissioned in 1963, and three years later HMS *Valiant* followed, the first to have a British-designed reactor. The Netherlands Navy considered the idea for a while but dropped it, leaving the French as the only other European Navy to adopt nuclear propulsion. The first French efforts were directed at establishing their SSBN force, and the first SSN was not laid down until 1972. Today the lead boat *Rubis* is in service and four more are in various stages of construction.

The Chinese have taken their time in building up a nuclear capability, but in 1974 it was reported that

Above: A Soviet Charlie class submarine whose 30-mile range SS-N-7 cruise missiles are seen as a potent threat to carrier battle groups.
Above left: The swans on the casing of *U.18* (left) and *U.17* show how small the German Type 206 submarines are.

the first of a class known as the *Han* had come into service. The existence of a second boat is doubtful, and trials of the first were reported to be very lengthy, suggesting an experimental prototype. Given the reluctance of the Chinese to sit back while potential enemies open the gap in technology still further, we can expect to see some sort of SSN and SSBN program before long.

From all this it might be assumed that there is no future for the diesel-electric submarine, but this is far from the case. Despite its awesome advantages of performance, the 'nuke' has certain limitations. Apart from the difficulties of communication already mentioned, she is a big sonar target and her bulk prevents her from venturing into coastal waters. She is inherently noisy, for her steam turbine machinery needs a gearbox to transmit power to the single shaft, and the reactor needs cooling pumps. Great efforts have been made in recent years to silence the machinery of nuclear submarines, primarily by isolating the machinery from the hull by putting it on a 'raft'. These expedients push up cost, of course, and also size; it has been admitted by the US Navy that silencing measures account for the fact that the *Los Angeles* class SSNs are over 2000 tons bigger than their predecessors, the *Sturgeon* class.

Some of the attempts to reduce noise have resulted in unorthodox solutions. In 1957 the USS *Seawolf* went to sea with her S2G reactor cooled by liquid sodium, the idea being to eliminate cooling pumps. It was not a success, and two years later the reactor was replaced by a pressurized water type similar to that in the *Nautilus*. The smaller SSN *Tullibee*, commissioned in 1960, used turbo-electric drive for the same reason, while the *Jack*, a member of the *Sturgeon* class was given contrarotating propellers and turbines. The newest British SSNs, the *Trafalgar* class, have a single pump-jet unit instead of the normal seven-bladed propeller; it reduces noise considerably, but at the cost of one or two knots' speed. Another aid to silent running is to cover the hull in anechoic tiling, which absorbs noise.

It was only a matter of time before Germany returned to the business of designing and building submarines. Once NATO agreed to the recreation of West German military forces the way was clear to develop a new generation of U-Boats, starting with three rehabilitated World War II hulls. A dozen Type 205 boats (*U.1-12*) were built by 1968. They were unusual in layout, with eight 21inch torpedo tubes forward, but on a surface displacement of only 370 tons they were so cramped that the torpedoes had to be loaded externally. The crew of 22 officers and men was made up entirely of specialists, who embarked only for the mission, much like aircrew. Apart from meals, little attention is paid to habitability; in harbor the crewmen are accommodated on board a tender.

SAPHIR

Some of the Type 205 U-Boats have since been scrapped, and the class was superseded by the 18 Type 206 (*U.13-30*), built in 1969–74. An increase in displacement of about 100 tons permitted a number of improvements, particularly another eight reload torpedoes. The design is particularly suited to the shallow, restricted waters of the Baltic, and similar submarines were built for Denmark and Norway, while a larger variant, the Type 209, has been sold to many countries. In the fighting around the Falklands the Argentine Navy's two Type 209 boats, the *Salta* and *San Luis* were reported to have made several attacks on the British Task Force. Reports suggest that one of the two submarines got near the British ships, but that her attack was frustrated by faulty torpedoes. According to one report no fewer than seven German SUT wire-guided torpedoes were fired but failed to explode (or were decoyed by British countermeasures). The manufacturers of the torpedo, AEG-Telefunken, claim that since the torpedoes were delivered in 1974 their engineers have not been allowed to inspect the submarines, and so they cannot be held responsible for any failure to keep the weapons or the fire control system in good condition. What is not in dispute is that the British had a healthy respect for the two Type 209s, and devoted a lot of attention to maintaining a tight antisubmarine screen at all times.

France has maintained a strong submarine force since the 1950s, when the losses of World War II were replaced. With a long Atlantic coastline to patrol there was a need for something larger than the German Baltic types, but the ten *Daphné* class of 1955–70 displaced only 700 tons on the surface, whereas the older *Narval* class displaced 1320 tons. The *Daphné* has proved popular with other navies, having been built for South Africa, Portugal, Spain and Pakistan, although it has also had its share of bad luck, with one

Main picture: HMS *Otter*, one of the British *Oberon* class submarines which have been sold to foreign navies. The 13 in service with the RN will eventually be replaced by the *Upholder* class.

Top left: The French nuclear attack submarine *Saphir*, second of the *Rubis* class, ready for launch at Cherbourg. These are the first SSNs built for the French Navy and a class of six is planned.

Above: A Soviet submarine sets out from an icy northern port. Above right: Soviet Type 641 boats, more commonly known by their NATO Foxtrot designation, in their base.

lost by accident. The Pakistani *Hangor* is also one of the few submarines to have seen action recently. She torpedoed the Indian frigate *Khukri* in 1971.

The latest diesel-electric submarines built in France are the four *Agosta* class, 1230-tonners armed with four 21.7-inch (550mm) torpedo tubes. The first export customer was South Africa, which ordered two in 1975, the *Adventurous* and *Astrant*, but when France enforced a United Nations embargo the two became the Pakistani *Hurmat* and *Hashmat*. Another four have been built in Spain by the same yard which built four *Daphnés*.

The Royal Netherlands Navy has built on the excellent reputation earned by its submarines and submariners in World War II. In 1949 Dutch designers produced an unusual triple-hulled design known as the *Potvis* class, in which the crew and torpedo tubes were housed in the uppermost cylinder, while batteries and propulsion were housed in two lower parallel cylinders. Four submarines were built to this design in 1954–66 but the novel arrangement was not repeated; although successful in providing extra diving depth it made for extremely complicated internal arrangements. The submarines most recently commissioned are the two *Zwaardvis* class, 2370-tonners armed with a combination of 20 Mk 48 torpedoes and Sub-Harpoon missiles. The US Navy provided some technical assistance, particularly by

making the plans of the *Barbel* class available.

The *Zwaardvis* design has been developed further, into the 2300-ton *Walrus* and *Zeeleeuw*, just coming into service. They differ mainly in being able to dive deeper, and in saving 18 men by a greater degree of automation. When the *Zeeleeuw* is operational the last of the *Potvis* class will be scrapped, to keep the force at four boats.

The Italians relied for some years on a quartet of 535-ton boats, the *Enrico Toti* class, and four elderly ex-American 'Guppy' Type submarines, but in 1974 the first of a new class of four, the *Nazario Sauro* was laid down. Like the Dutch boats they have benefited from American experience with the *Barbel* class, but are armed with Italian A-184 torpedoes. Once all four are operational the American 'Guppies' will be returned, and another four submarines may be built to replace the *Enrico Toti* class.

Although strictly neutral and non-aligned, the Royal Swedish Navy has not neglected submarine developments and has produced a series of advanced designs. The oldest boats in service are the six *Draken* class, 835-ton boats built in 1959–62 and armed with 12 torpedoes. Since then six *Sjoormen* class (Type 11B) have been built, followed by three *Näcken* class (Type 14). These last two classes have some unusual features: a stubby hull and X-form diving planes aft. Being designed for the Baltic they have a relatively shallow diving depth, 150 meters, and in the *Näcken* class a high degree of automation has reduced the crew to only 19 officers and men.

The next design on the drawing board is the A17

S61

Above: The Spanish *Delphin* on trials, one of the four French *Daphné* type built under license in Spain.
Left: A Foxtrot class diesel/electric submarine with a Kashin class DDG in the background.

Type or *Västergötland* class. Although basically similar to the *Näcken* design they will rely even more heavily on automation. For a long time it was hoped to use an unorthodox method of powering the *Västergötland* class, either a closed-cycle Stirling engine (using no atmospheric oxygen) or fuel cells, but progress with these two interesting ideas was too slow and so costly that it is certain that the existing type of diesel-electric motors will be continued.

Sweden has pursued her own ideas in torpedo design as well. When in 1956 the British submarine *Sidon* blew up in Portland Harbor the fault was traced to hydrogen peroxide, used as a propellant in the Mk 12 'Fancy' torpedo. The Swedes asked for and were given access to the design and the enquiry which followed the *Sidon* incident. Out of this emerged the Tp 61 wire-guided torpedo, which has reportedly never had a single accident in 10,000 runs.

Even a country with a small industrial base, like Yugoslavia, can develop her own submarines. The *Sutjeska* and *Neretva* (1957–62) were the first submarines to be built locally, and they have been followed by three *Heroj* class (1965–70) and two *Sava* class (1975–80). It is assumed that some Soviet technical aid has been supplied, but Yugoslavian surface warships use Western equipment as well, and the current submarines bear no resemblance to individual Russian designs.

The British, faced with the cost of maintaining a comparatively large force of SSNs and SSBNs (16 by 1981) had made up their minds that the 13 *Oberon* and three remaining *Porpoise* class diesel-electric boats would not be replaced when they wore out in the 1980s. However the growing difficulties of manning SSNs and the realization that SSNs could not provide sufficiently accurate inshore surveillance led to a new Naval Staff Requirement (NSR) for an SSK or *Oberon* Replacement in the mid-1980s. This has now been ordered as the *Upholder* class, and the prototype is expected to join the Fleet in 1988.

The *Upholder* class derives many of its design features, particularly the hull form, from the most recent SSNs, although it is of course, much smaller. The emphasis is on weapons and fire control, rather than maximum range and performance; they are designed for 20 knots on the surface and submerged, and carry 18 Spearfish torpedoes or Sub-Harpoon missiles (six in the tubes and 12 reloads). The 21-inch Spearfish is the replacement for the Mk 24 Tigerfish, and because it is intended to match the latest Russian SSNs has been designed to dive down to 3000 feet and run at 55 knots. To achieve such remarkable performance the designers abandoned electric batteries in favor of a compact Sundstrand turbine running on enriched Otto fuel, and on trials one of the test vehicles is reported to have exceeded 72 knots while running on the surface (the extra margin is necessary to guarantee 55 knots at maximum depth).

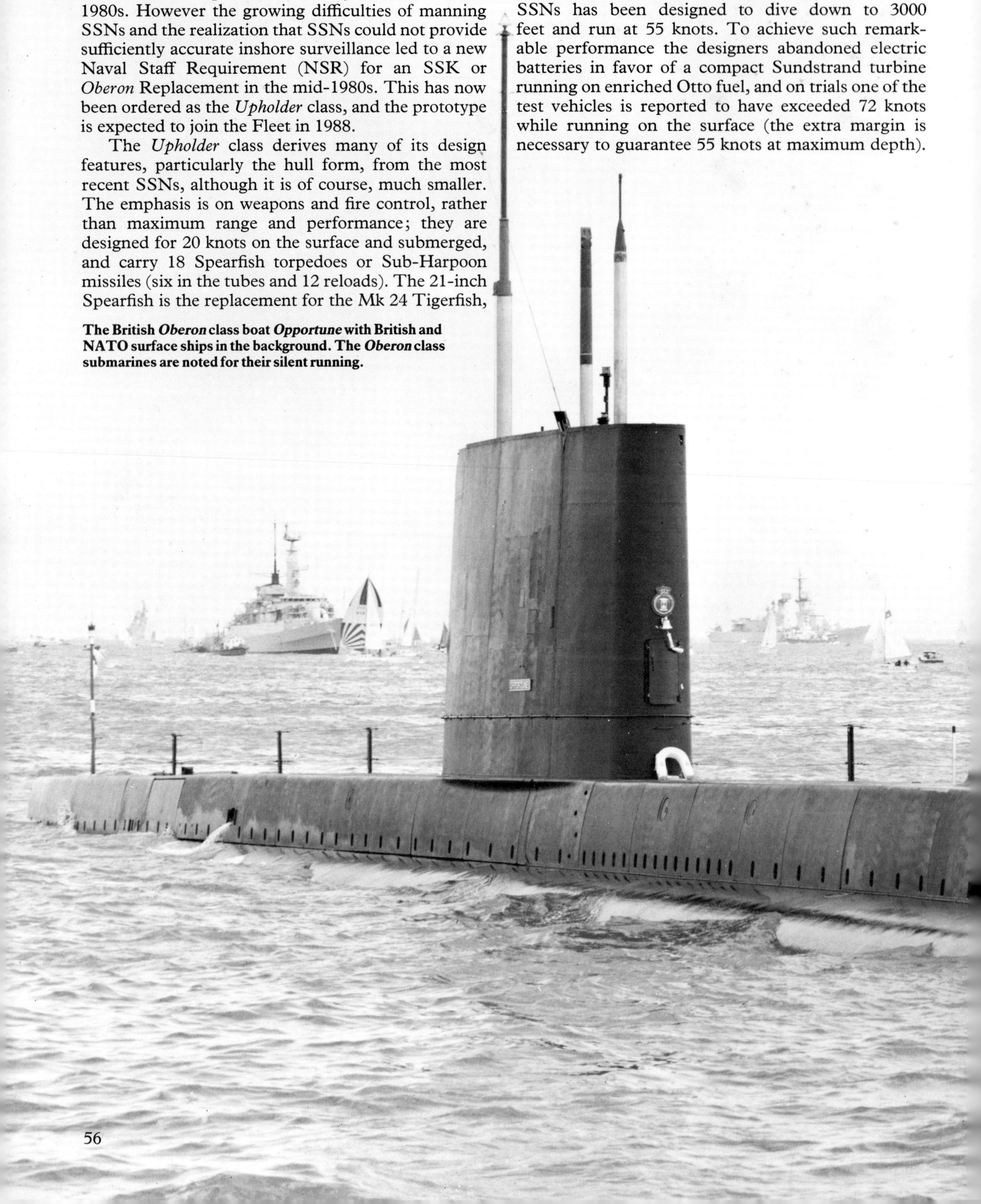

The British *Oberon* class boat *Opportune* with British and NATO surface ships in the background. The *Oberon* class submarines are noted for their silent running.

The weapons ranged against submarines are formidable. To match the long detection ranges achieved by modern sonars the antisubmarine weapons have had to extend their range. Against the ships which launch such weapons the submarine can fire a torpedo or antiship missile, but against its most numerous and persistent enemy, the helicopter with a dipping sonar and lightweight torpedoes, there is no easy response. Some years ago a British company produced a solution known as the Submarine Launched Airflight Missile or SLAM, using four small Blowpipe missiles in a special launcher which retracted into the fin, like a periscope or snorkel mast. Guidance was by a TV link, with the operator guiding the missile from a monitor down below in the control room. SLAM worked, and the Israeli Navy even went so far as to fit their submarines for it but it had one great disadvantage; no submarine commander is happy about loitering at periscope depth when he knows that helicopters are in the vicinity. Helicopters are such a threat to submarines that it can only be a matter of time before a countermeasure is developed, but for the moment the main defense is to avoid them, and this is usually done by tracking the emissions from their radars and sonars. All modern submarines have an Electronic Support Measures (ESM) mast fitted with receiving aerials to measure and analyze signals above water; as ESM is passive a submarine can put up a mast before surfacing, to make sure that there is no threat nearby.

The Soviet Navy, as we have already seen, embraced the idea of the nuclear hunter-killer submarine, building the Tango class to follow the Novembers and Victors, but what caused more alarm in Western navies was the appearance of attack submarines armed with cruise missiles. The earliest were somewhat crude, the diesel-electric Juliett class in the early 1960s, which could fire SS-N-3 missiles on the surface. Much more potent, however, was the Charlie class SSN with its ability to hit surface warships such as aircraft carriers with their SS-N-7 missiles from a range of 30 miles. The risk is that a submarine with such a missile can close within the antisubmarine screen, so that the missile 'pops up' well inside the screen around the carrier. Such an attack stands a good chance of overwhelming the normal defenses in depth, leaving the target nothing but last ditch defenses against the missile.

Clearly the Soviet Navy found the idea of an SSGN (nuclear submarine, guided missile) attractive; the Charlie II is believed to have eight SS-N-9 missiles, with possibly double the range of the

31
594

The USS *Permit* (SSN.594) loading a Subroc missile through her torpedo loading hatch. Subroc has a nuclear depth charge warhead and is fired from underwater. It exits and becomes airborne before re-entering the water in the target area.

SS-N-7. Two more SSGN classes have been reported, a single Papa class and the Oscar class.

Soviet naval planners are believed to favor a 'high-low mix' of capability, and in line with a policy of building high-value SSNs they have continued to build SSKs in large numbers. The majority of the diesel-electric boats of the 1950s have been scrapped, put into reserve or relegated to training, but 20 Romeo class were completed in 1958–61, to complement the 60 Foxtrot type completed in the late 1950s. The 2000-ton Foxtrot is seen all around the world and has been supplied to a number of foreign countries as a replacement for obsolete Whiskey boats. A total of 74 Romeos was built in China to Soviet plans, and a derivative, the Ming class, is reported. In October 1981 one of the dwindling number of Whiskey class, *No. 137*, achieved notoriety by running ashore in the approaches to the Swedish Navy's main base at Karlskrona. The luckless captain claimed that a faulty echo sounder had led him astray, following a navigation error which put him somewhere off the coast of Poland! Subsequently the Swedes claimed that they had detected radiation, and suggested that *No. 137* was armed with nuclear torpedoes, something which is hard to reconcile with the great age of the Whiskey.

Clearly in wartime both nuclear and conventional submarines have important roles to play in Soviet strategy. The SSNs and SSGNs would have the primary task of attacking the West's Sea Lanes of Communications (SLOCs), to prevent the United States and its allies from deploying their military power at will. Neutralization of the Carrier Battle Groups and Surface Action Groups would be another priority, using both torpedoes and missiles. The longer ranged missiles might well be supplied with target data from long range maritime patrol aircraft or surface ships. The North Atlantic SLOCs are likely to be the main objective, for through these crowded shipping lanes would have to pass the vital convoys of war materiel, ammunition and fuel to resupply Europe.

Fortunately for the NATO alliance geography still constrains the Russians in the same way that it did France and Germany in previous wars. The shallow waters of the Baltic have only one narrow exit to the open sea, and that is securely guarded by the naval and air forces of Norway, West Germany and Denmark. This leaves the burden of attack to the Northern Fleet, based on Murmansk, and from there all Soviet forces must run the gauntlet of surveillance by NATO forces long before they reach the North Atlantic hunting grounds. Even then the exit to the Atlantic is blocked by Iceland and the British Isles, for submarines could not hope to transit the English Channel or the Irish Sea. Hence the vital importance of the Greenland–Iceland–UK Gap (usually abbreviated to the GIUK Gap). It is a 'choke point' through which Soviet submarines *must* pass if they are to fulfil

Top: *U.24*(S.173) one of the 18 Type 206 submarines built for the Federal German Navy in the 1960s.
Above: The Victor class was the second Soviet class of SSN to come into service.
Below: A touching reunion for a Soviet officer, presumably from the Foxtrot submarine in the background.

their main missions, and therefore NATO concentrates its ASW forces in that area.

The major problem in hunting submarines is to narrow down the area of search, in order to eliminate the largely futile effort of spreading ships, aircraft and hunter-killer submarines over a wide area. This was done in the 1960s by laying a series of antisubmarine barriers in the GIUK Gap. This is a series of passive sensors on the bed of the ocean which are linked by cable to shore stations in Iceland, Northern Ireland, England and Scotland. The system, which is constantly being refined, is known as the SOund SUrveillance System or SOSUS, and its existence was a well-kept secret until the mid-1970s. Briefly its passive sensors record the passage of any surface ship or submarine within audible range, and relay it to a shore station; there computers rapidly triangulate the submarine's position from the various bearings, classify the submarine as 'friendly' or 'hostile', and direct friendly forces to the location.

What makes SOSUS effective is the rapidity of modern electronics; within microseconds the 'library' of individual propeller noises is scanned, to identify the submarine by nationality, class, and even in some cases, down to an individual boat. Equally quickly the forces in the GIUK Gap are alerted to the presence of, say, a third November class SSN.

There are many SOSUS barriers, all at strategic positions, where the right combinations of topography force hostile submarines through a predictable channel. Special weapons have been developed for these barriers, particularly the Captor mine; in essence it is a canister containing an acoustic homing torpedo such as the Mk 46, which is launched automatically on 'hearing' the noise of an approaching submarine. Captor is intended to catch submarines diving deep to avoid detection by the sonars and sonobuoys of ships and aircraft above.

Clearly the existence of such barriers imposes severe limits on Soviet plans to use their submarines decisively, and almost certainly the Alfa class nuclear submarine was one such solution. In 1980 reports began to filter through to the Western press, suggesting that a new type of Soviet submarine could make 40 knots and dive to well over 2000ft. According to 'well-informed sources' American and British submarines had tailed these new SSNs and had lost them at an estimated 40 knots. Known as the Alfa by NATO, the new craft is an SSN, credited with a surface displacement of 2600 tons and an armament of six 21-inch torpedo tubes firing a 'mix' of six long range torpedoes, 10 short range antisubmarine torpedoes, two nuclear-tipped torpedoes, two nuclear antisubmarine missiles and two conventional antisubmarine missiles.

Such a heavy armament is by no means unusual, and conforms to the Soviet tendency towards maximum weapon-load, but it leaves some questions unanswered. At maximum depth weapon launching would be so dangerous as to be almost impossible, and sonars and homing heads would have great difficulty in identifying targets on the surface. The Alfa must therefore be assumed to require its immense speed to pass through SOSUS barriers at maximum depth, in effect outflanking the defending forces. If this theory is right, her armament would only be used at a later stage, when she had reached her patrol area.

Some observers ask how the size of the Alfa has come *down* from the 4000 tons of the Charlie class and yet must have doubled the power output to increase speed from 30 knots. One explanation may be that the Soviet designers have simply chosen to ignore the normal safety limits on reactor output in order to achieve a decisive margin of speed. There are persistent rumors that the Alfa prototype had to be scrapped after the reactor had suffered a 'melt-down' – with the loss of her entire crew. The resistance of the hull to pressure at maximum depth is apparently the result of using a double titanium hull – an immensely expensive way to build a submarine, but understandable as titanium is much lighter than steel. Certainly the double hull would make the Alfa resistant to a hit from a typical Western light torpedo such as the Mk 46, which has only 75 pounds of explosive, designed to knock off a propeller. The next generation of NATO submarine torpedoes have a heavy warhead to ensure a 'first-time kill' – something which is absolutely necessary when attacking an SSBN. It is easy to imagine the captain of an SSBN realizing that his boat had been crippled, and giving the order to fire his deadly load of missiles as a last act of defiance.

The underwater battlefield will be one of the most crucial, even decisive. It will be a campaign of ambush and sudden catastrophe, with a clear-cut distinction between survivors and non-survivors.

The USS *John F. Kennedy*'s air group practically obscures her flight deck. US aircraft carriers cannot accommodate their entire aircraft complement in the hangar.

4. SURFACE COMBAT

In the final analysis surface warfare is the most important element of naval conflict, at least for those navies with an interest in 'power-projection'. Put at its simplest, men and some equipment can be flown rapidly from one continent to another, but heavy materials must go by sea; if they cannot cross that sea because of enemy action they cannot influence the outcome of any events away from their homeland. From this simple fact stems the concept of 'Sea Control' as against 'Sea Denial'; sea control is needed to move not only military equipment but vital raw materials, aid to allies, etc, and an enemy who lacks such control can only attempt to deny the use of the sea.

The outcome of two world wars hinged on sea control, for in 1917 and 1942–43 the United States was very nearly prevented from supporting its ally Great Britain because Anglo-American sea control was threatened by German sea denial forces in the form of U-Boats. Since 1945 the United States and its allies have enjoyed undisputed control of the sea, but the growing Soviet Navy created under the leadership of Admiral Gorshkov poses a very real threat of sea denial. Added to that is an enormous increase in the potential of the submarine and the aircraft, to the point where some commentators question the ability of the surface fleet to survive at all.

The US Navy's response is to state categorically that it intends to retain control of the sea, and that it will pay the higher price of sea power. It can very easily be forgotten that the West currently has only two means of taking the offensive at sea: with attack submarines or carrier air strikes, so any abdication from surface warfare would free powerful Russian forces to act against Western sea communications.

Today the defense of a surface fleet against air-flight weapons, whether launched from aircraft, ships or submarines has to be in 'layers'. The outermost layer is provided by fleet interceptor aircraft, using their own radars and those of the carrier battle group to provide a complete picture of the area and to make accurate interceptions. Ideally these interceptors will be able to destroy hostile aircraft before they can launch their antiship missiles, using air-to-air missiles or guns. The next layer of defense is provided by the fleet's missiles, which provide 'area defense'; they can shoot down the larger and slower antiship missiles as well as the launching aircraft. Any aircraft which 'leak' past these two layers are to be dealt with by the so-called 'point defense' systems mounted in individual ships.

The concept of layered defense was developed in the later 1950s to cope with bomber-launched missiles and the early Soviet long range cruise missiles such as the SS-N-3 and the later SS-N-12, in open waters. In narrow waters, however there is always the risk that the long range defenses can be bypassed, by fast strike craft firing SS-N-2 Styx or SS-N-9 missiles. A further complication was the appearance of the Charlie class submarine firing SS-N-7 missiles from underwater. This missile could, for example, 'pop up' from a submerged submarine only 25 miles from its target. Traveling at one-and-a-half times the speed of sound an SS-N-7 would cover that distance in about 90 seconds, giving the target ship's defenses very little time to react. Nor can the missile be allowed to approach too close, for even if the guidance system is destroyed by hits on the nose cone there is a risk that the missile will 'go ballistic' and hit the ship. Even if the warhead fails to detonate, the impact of a ton or more of missile body will inflict massive damage on the superstructure of a warship and will knock out her radars, so the only valid defense is to prevent missiles from getting close.

The current family of US Navy missiles are descendants of the 'Bumblebee Project' of 1944, when the Applied Physics Laboratory of Johns Hopkins University started the development of stand-off defenses agsinst the early German antiship missiles such as Fx-1400. Out of this came the 'Three-T' surface-to-air missiles, Talos, Terrier and Tartar. The very long range Talos (70 miles) has now been retired, but Terrier proved to be the basis for continuing development, and is still in service. An attempt in the mid-1950s to produce an ultra-long range defense system, Typhon, foundered when size and cost ran out of control, but experience gained helped to get the current Aegis program under way.

The close range guns of World War II were inadequate to cope with fast aircraft, even in 1945, and so they disappeared. However missiles were found to have minimum ranges as well as maximum, and as data-handling has improved radically since the 1950s guns are back in favor as short range defensive systems.

The Soviet Navy differs from the US Navy in concentrating its air element on land, rather than in aircraft carriers. The central philosophy of tying the airborne striking forces to bases in the Soviet Union may change, but for the moment the Soviet Navy lacks the ability to project power on a large scale, and so it remains committed to a role of sea denial. The evidence that this philosophy is undergoing change is the building of what is believed to be a 60,000-ton carrier, probably nuclear-powered, but one carrier will not be a match for the US Navy, and the real question must be, how far will the Soviet Navy go down this new path?

The importance attached by Soviet leaders to the Strategic Rocket Forces has in the past hampered a coherent development of naval strategy. The first heavy cruise missile, the SS-N-3, was developed originally for strategic attack, but was retailored to permit attacks against US carriers.

Even the construction of strategic missile-firing submarines was suspended at one time, to avoid any

Ships of the NATO STANAVFORLANT (Standing Naval Force, Atlantic) a multi-national force of escorts.

suggestion that the Soviet Navy might be overlapping the mission of the Strategic Rocket Forces. Only after the downfall of Nikita Krushchev, the most fervent admirer of the SRF, and the advent of Polaris did the Navy begin to win back some ground in the battle for funds.

By 1973 the voice of Admiral Gorshkov could be heard, delineating the new power projection role for the Navy. In his book *Sea Power of the State* he suggested that in the future only a powerful and balanced Navy would be able to guarantee Soviet influence in the Third World. While dismissing the role of sea power in World War II (the standard Soviet line is that their land forces alone defeated Nazi Germany, and that the war in the Pacific was irrelevant) Gorshkov predicted that missiles and nuclear weapons were altering the very nature of naval warfare.

The new policy took several forms. The new Backfire bomber began to appear in numbers, and a steady series of classes of 'rocket cruisers' began to join the Fleet. In 1976 the *Kiev* appeared, an unusual hybrid cruiser/carrier capable of operating the Yak-36 Forger vertical takeoff strike aircraft. With her sisters *Minsk* and later *Novorossiisk*, as well as two earlier helicopter carriers, it seemed as if the Soviet Navy was rapidly expanding its anticarrier capability, and the appearance of a 22,000-ton 'battlecruiser', the *Kirov*, was taken to herald the imminent appearance of carrier battle groups in hitherto sacrosanct NATO areas. However, at the time of writing the carrier has not appeared and observers are beginning to reassess the significance of current Soviet building programs.

The four Kynda class were the first purpose-built guided missile ships, although previously the somewhat primitive SS-N-1 Scrubber missile had been added to existing destroyer designs, the Kildin and Krupny classes. With a long forecastle, two large funnels and massive radar arrays, the Kynda class made a great impression on Western and Third World observers, but in particular their eight massive launch tubes containing SS-N-3 Shaddock missiles marked

Main picture: The experimental hydrofoil USS *High Point* firing a Harpoon antiship missile.
Top right: Following trials with the *High Point* and other vessels, a class of six missile hydrofoils (PHMs) was built for the US Navy. The *Taurus* (PHM.3) is seen running trials in Elliot Bay, Washington.
Below: A Soviet Osa II class missile boat, one of a large number of missile craft built in the late 1950s, many of which have been transferred to friendly navies.

them as powerful surface combatants. Unlike contemporary Western warships the Kyndas were bristling with weapons, a further eight Shaddock reloads, a twin launcher for SA-N-1 Goa antiaircraft missiles, two twin 76mm guns and two sets of triple torpedo tubes. All this, and an estimated speed of 35 knots achieved on a full load displacement calculated at 5700 tons, suggested to Western observers that the Soviets were more skilful at designing warships.

The perspective of nearly 25 years (the first Kynda appeared as long ago as 1961) suggests a different view. The sea trials almost certainly revealed significant defects, which were mitigated by reconstruction to reduce topweight, but the ships were still sent to the Black Sea and Pacific squadrons, where they faced less demanding weather. Even more significant, the class was cut from 12 to four units, and the next class mounted a smaller number of missiles. This was the so called Kresta I class, the first of which appeared in 1967, six years after the first Kynda.

Although hailed at the time as another leap ahead for the Soviet fleet, sober opinion now sees the Kresta I as a worthy attempt to correct the deficiencies of the Kynda. The number of SS-N-3 Shaddock missiles was cut from 16 to 4, a reduction of 75 percent, and a

Above: The Swedish patrol boat *Piteå* is the test ship for the new RBS.15 antiship missile.
Below: The Soviet *Komar* Class were the world's first missile-armed strike craft.

Above: The Israeli *Reshef* class carry Gabriel and Harpoon missiles and 76mm guns.
Below: The Danish *Willemoes* class were armed with 21-inch torpedoes and a 76mm gun but now carry four Harpoons.

helicopter was included to provide mid-course guidance for the 170-mile Shaddock. Instead a second twin launcher for SA-N-1 Goa area defense missiles and a long range air surveillance radar were provided. Once again, however, only four were built before another major shift in policy supervened. Fortunately for the Russians the basic Kresta hull could be adapted, and so in 1970 a Kresta II appeared.

What distinguished the cruiser *Kronshtadt* from her earlier sisters was the redesigned central tower superstructure to accommodate a three dimensional radar, linked to the new SA-N-3 Goblet area defense missile system, of which two systems were provided. Another important change was to replace the two twin Shaddock missile tubes with two quadruple launchers for a new type of large missile. For seven years Western intelligence maintained that these were a new long range cruise missile designated SS-N-10, but finally it was revealed to be a comparatively short range antisubmarine missile designated SS-N-14 – in effect a pilotless delivery vehicle for a homing torpedo. This squared more believably with the Russians' own designation of the ships as Large Anti Submarine Ships but it also implied a drastic revision of Soviet ideas on fleet distribution, for these big ships (7500 tons full load) have no gun bigger than 57mm and no antiship missile, apparently.

The Kresta II does, however, appear to meet Soviet needs, for no fewer than ten were built between 1970 and 1978, and they have been seen around the world. While they were still under construction yet another type of missile cruiser appeared, the 9000-ton Kara. Although bearing a superficial likeness to the Kresta II, they complemented them rather than replaced them, and the *rationale* seems to be a wish to exploit higher technology in propulsion and weapons, but without interrupting the flow of ships from the Black Sea shipyards.

The big difference is the adoption of gas turbines for the Kara, most probably four 'marinized' versions of the NK-144 turbines which powered the Tu-144 'Concordski' supersonic airliner. This allowed the designers to use a big square upright funnel set well back, in place of the complex 'mack' used in both Kresta types. Although the armament remains similar to the Kresta II, eight SS-N-14 missiles forward and twin SA-N-3 Goblet SAMs forward and aft, a new point defense system is installed amidships, the twin SA-N-4 missile. These are housed to port and starboard in twin 'pop-up' launchers to protect them from spray. Also mounted on either side amidships are a pair of twin 76mm guns and four six-barreled 23mm 'Gatling' guns for close range defense against aircraft and missiles.

If the succession of Kyndas, Krestas and Karas from Soviet shipyards provoked unease it was nothing compared to the explosion of analytical comment set off by the appearance of the cruiser/carrier *Kiev* in 1976. It was partly her massive size, 40,000 tons full load, but in particular her port-side angled flight deck and general aircraft carrier characteristics which provoked disquiet. Immediately specters were raised of *Kiev* and her sisters combining with the helicopter carriers *Moskva* and *Leningrad* to form a powerful task force in the Arabian Sea ready to threaten the West's vital oil supplies.

181

In fact the *Kiev*, *Minsk* and *Novorossiisk* (plus a fourth sister *Kharkov*, believed to be ready for sea in 1985) bear only a superficial resemblance to the US Navy's carriers. They have very few of their capabilities, lacking specific airborne early warning (AEW) or electronic warfare (EW) functions. The air group is particularly weak: 18–24 Ka-25 Hormone antisubmarine helicopters and some 10–12 Yak-36 Forger VTOL strike aircraft. The Hormone-A is a small elderly helicopter with half the range of the Western Sea King, and much less than the S-3 Viking ASW aircraft. The Yak-36 Forger squadron, should it try to attack an American carrier battle group, would face three attack and two interceptor squadrons of vastly superior performance. Nor, without AEW, could the Forgers be vectored out in time to fight off a determined air strike, and it seems they would be restricted to shooting down reconnaissance aircraft or dealing with small strike craft.

Above: Artist's impression of the nuclear-powered cruiser *Kirov*. Apart from aircraft carriers the *Kirov* is the largest warship to be built since the battleships of World War II.
Left: The *Kirov* heels to port during a high speed turn. The *Kirov* may have a top speed as high as 35 knots.
Right: Detail of the forward parts of the *Kirov* showing the oblique launch tubes for the SS-N-19 missiles (shown below) and the vertical tubes for the SA-N-6 (above). Forward of these is the twin SS-N-14 equipment.
Below: Missile hatches on the foredeck of the *Kirov*. Also shown are four of the ship's eight 30mm Gatling-type guns and (left) the tops of the retractable SA-N-4 mountings.

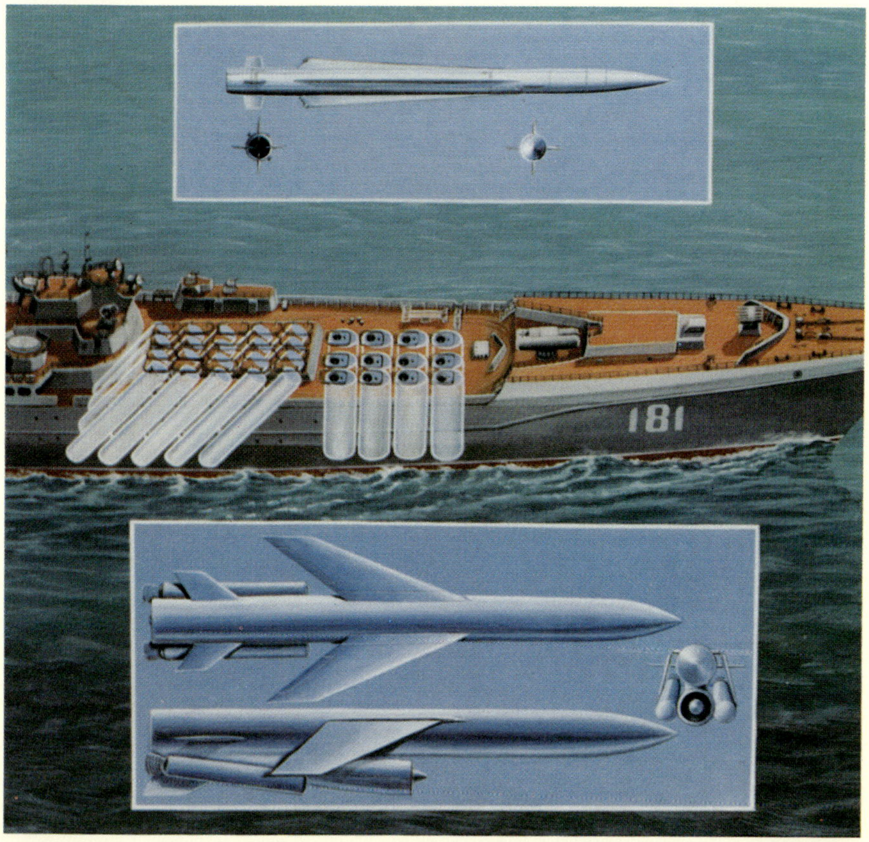

Above: Two Turya class torpedo-armed hydrofoils en route to Cuba as deck cargo on a Soviet merchant ship.

Right: Stern view of the British DLG *Bristol*, showing the large dome covering the Type 909 tracker radar.

Nor can it be said that the hybrid cruiser/carrier hull contributes much to efficiency as a carrier. Only 50 percent of the ship is dedicated to air capability, for the entire forward part of the hull and much of the island superstructure is dedicated to the various cruiser functions. The armament duplicates that of the Kara, and in addition to at least eight long range SS-N-12 antiship missiles, the island superstructure is cluttered with sensors and weapons as well as fire control to handle the various weapon systems, making it quite clear that the 'cruiser' part of the design ranks equal to the 'carrier' function.

Current thinking is that the *Kiev* class is only a logical step in the evolution of Soviet naval doctrine. Great stress is laid on the role of long range reconnaissance bombers, the Blinders, Badgers and Bears, acting in concert with surface units and submarines. Their task is to provide data for a central bank of information about Western naval movements known as the Soviet Ocean Surveillance System (SOSS). The Bear-D is one of the key elements in this set-up, and it is intended to act as a relay station for long range missiles such as the SS-N-3. Ideally the Bear-D will locate a hostile task force, call down fire from any available air strike squadrons and surface ships, and take over midcourse guidance of the missiles to direct them onto their targets. Hormone-B helicopters can provide mid-course guidance for anti-ship missiles.

Until the advent of Polaris in the early 1960s the major function of Soviet forces in mid-ocean was to force the US carrier task forces out to a range at which their nuclear strike aircraft could not hit targets in the USSR. The existence of Polaris changed all this, for the Soviet Navy now had to try to hunt SSBNs out to new ranges, 1500 miles for A-2, and then to 2500 miles when the A-3 replaced the A-2 Polaris. This fact alone accounts for the profusion of antisubmarine weapons in the Kresta II, Kara and *Kiev* classes, and the increased number of 'blue water' combatants, for these antisubmarine forces would be operating much closer to hostile forces. What was also noticeable was a shift in the emphasis on the four Soviet fleets. Western SSBNs were to be covered by stronger ASW forces in the Northern Atlantic and the Mediterranean, and to build up the strength of the Northern and Black Sea Fleets the Baltic and Pacific Fleets were weakened.

The need to push antisubmarine forces further and further into the oceans has put great pressure on the Soviet Navy to produce a series of cruisers capable of defending themselves from heavy attack. Each class of cruiser has been larger and more powerful than the last, but apart from the Kynda, Kresta I and *Kiev* classes, the emphasis has been on ASW weapons at the expense of antiship weapons. Nor could helicopters and single bombers offer much chance of being allowed to loiter around an American carrier battle group broadcasting target data. Clearly what was needed was a large surface combatant capable of challenging NATO and the Americans in the open waters of the North Atlantic and the Norwegian Sea.

The solution was the 22,000-ton 'battlecruiser' *Kirov*, which appeared in 1981. However, even on such a large platform the designers have had difficulty in providing a massive increase in offensive power, for the defenses of the ship had to be increased as well. Thus the *Kirov* mounts only four more antiship missiles than the Kynda (20 as against 16); the rest of the 247-meter hull is taken up with stowage for as many as 60 SA-N-6 antiaircraft missiles, SS-N-14 antisubmarine missiles, SA-N-4 point defense missiles, 30mm 'Gatlings' and a large number of fire control sets, surveillance radars and the comprehensive outfit of ECM gear necessary for survival. What is unusual is the choice of vertical launching for both the SS-N-19 and the SA-N-6 missiles – a concept long discussed in the West but slow in appearing because of the technical difficulties.

The most controversial aspect of the *Kirov*'s design was her propulsion, and it must be confessed that Western Intelligence did not show up well by predicting that she was driven by a nuclear powerplant. The sight of what was clearly a massive combined mast/funnel or 'mack' emitting smoke was airily dismissed by some intelligence sources as a dummy, or else an exhaust trunk for auxiliary generators. Gradually, however, everyone came to accept that the likeliest explanation is that *Kirov* uses nuclear power for cruising, with oil-fired boilers providing boost power for rapid acceleration and top speed. In fact this CONAS (Combined Nuclear And Steam) had previously been proposed for US surface combatants as a way to solve the sluggish acceleration of nuclear plants, and it is easy to understand why it has been chosen by the Russian ship designers.

Although the *Kirov* incorporates many ideas new to Soviet warships she represents in one sense the final attempt to build a surface combatant capable of autonomous operation in hostile waters – autonomous in the sense of not relying on air support. The hazards of making a 2000-mile voyage from Murmansk down to the Denmark Strait are considerable, and it is unlikely that a ship making that passage would go completely undetected by modern surveillance systems. Should she attempt to make it the *Kirov* will need every defensive system she has to survive, and that knowledge is likely to have assisted the Soviet Navy in reaching the conclusion that it needs the protection of carrier air power.

Against this array of ships is ranged the might of the US Navy's surface fleet, assisted by the rest of the NATO allies' navies. However the US Navy's 14 large strike carriers provide all the 'muscle', as all other surface combatants are primarily designed to work with and protect the carriers. The carriers changed their designation from 'attack' (CVA) to CV some years ago, in recognition of the growing need to embark antisubmarine helicopters and aircraft, but the major element in the carriers' air groups is still strike and interceptor aircraft.

The oldest US carriers are the 63,600-ton *Midway* and *Coral Sea*, completed shortly after World War II but massively modernized since then. Although in 1949 the US Navy lost its fight to build a new carrier to be called the *United States*, experience in the Korean War led to the decision being reversed, and in 1956–59 four 'super carriers' of the *Forrestal* class joined the Fleet. These giant carriers displace 78,700 tons fully loaded, and they have proved so successful that the basis of US carrier design has remained largely constant since then. Four more improved versions followed, the *Kitty Hawk* class, but to explore the possibilities of nuclear propulsion the 82,000-ton *Enterprise* was built in 1958–61.

The use of nuclear propulsion in an attack carrier opened up new possibilities in surface warfare. Not only does the carrier have much greater endurance, but also greater fuel capacity for air operations, as her internal volume is not given up to 2–3000 tons of oil fuel. In fact all subsequent improvements to US carriers have gone on extending the time that the air group can keep flying, and enhancing the air group's efficiency.

Congress tried to keep the cost of naval aviation down by blocking funds for more nuclear carriers but

P 967

P411

Left: The *Skudd*, one of the Royal Norwegian Navy's *Storm* class strike craft, fires a Penguin sea-skimming missile.
Bottom left: Small navies have a peacetime need for lightly armed patrol boats such as the Mauritanian Republic's *le Dix Juillet*, but in an emergency such craft can be equipped with light missiles.
Below: The Royal Thai Navy has 3 Italian-built, Exocet-armed, *Ratcharit* strike craft and they are being joined by two larger gunboats.

each time the logic of the argument won through, and in 1968 the first of three more nuclear carriers was laid down. The *Nimitz* (CVN.68), *Dwight D Eisenhower* (CVN.69) and *Carl Vinson* (CVN.70) are now in service, with two more under construction, to replace the ageing *Midway* and *Coral Sea*. The full load displacement has risen to 93,400 tons but improvements in nuclear technology mean that they can make 35 knots with only two reactors, as against eight in the *Enterprise*. The age of the *Forrestals* has been a cause of concern but they have been earmarked for a Service Life Extension Program which will add 10–15 years to their lives. This involves major overhauls of the hull and machinery, rather than an update of their electronics and hardware, for the hulls are now 30 years old.

Modern carriers carry very little in the way of defensive armament, usually point defense missile launchers or the new 20mm Phalanx 'Gatling' gun, capable of firing 3000 rounds per minute against missiles. Defense at any greater distance is left to escorts, and of course the carrier's own aircraft. The all-important second layer of air defense is provided by guided missile armed destroyers (DDGs) and cruisers (CGs), armed with area defense weapons. The backbone of the carrier escort force is the *Charles F Adams* class of 23 DDGs, armed with the Standard medium range missile. They were built in 1959–63 and have proved very successful in service. They are good general purpose escorts as well, for in addition to their Standard missile systems they can fire Asroc antisubmarine missiles and Harpoon antiship missiles. When built they had two single 5-inch Mk 42 dual-purpose guns but one of these has been removed during modernization.

Similar to the *Adams* class in configuration are the ten DDGs of the *Coontz* class, but they displace 1300 tons more. They were built in 1957–61 as missile-armed destroyer leaders (DLGs) but were later downgraded to destroyers. Apart from size they differ from

the DDGs principally in being armed with the Terrier missile, which is being replaced by the Standard (Extended Range) missile. They have their missile launchers and fire control aft, and the Asroc antisubmarine missile system forward.

Despite being guided by radar, antiaircraft missiles have blind arcs, like other weapons, and the successors to the *Coontz* class DLGs were intended to be 'double-enders', with missile systems forward and aft to cure this problem. Two somewhat similar classes were built in 1959–67, nine *Leahy* class and nine *Belknaps*. They were also armed with Terrier SAMs and Asroc, but in recent years they have been given Harpoon antiship missiles as well, and are receiving Standard (ER) missiles in place of Terrier.

Although the nuclear-powered *Enterprise* was a great success she imposed a great strain on her 'fossil-fueled' escorts, as they had to refuel frequently. The answer was to build a series of nuclear-powered escorts, capable of keeping pace with her. The cruiser *Long Beach* was completed in 1961, a 17,350-ton ship armed with a twin Talos launcher and two twin Terrier launchers. To give her maximum flexibility it was originally planned to give her Regulus II cruise missiles, and when the program was canceled, Polaris ballistic missiles, but that system was deleted to save money. Although more than halfway through effective life she has been modernized, with Talos removed, Terriers replaced by Standard (ER) missiles and Harpoon antiship missiles added.

The *Long Beach* was followed by two more nuclear 'frigates' or DLGs built between 1962 and 1967, the *Bainbridge* and *Truxtun*, both armed with Terrier and Asroc missiles. They were experimental ships, basically enlarged versions of the *Leahy* and *Belknap* classes, and in 1975 they were all upgraded to guided missile cruisers (CGs and CGNs). The decision to build more nuclear carriers inevitably led to the construction of more CGNs, starting with the two *California* class and leading on to the four *Virginia*

A typical NATO escort group, showing (left to right) a Norwegian *Oslo* class destroyer escort, a Dutch *Leander* class frigate, the American DDG *Luce*, a British *Leander*, and a Canadian destroyer escort.

Above: The nuclear-powered missile cruiser *Bainbridge* (CGN.25) at sea in 1979.
Left: HMS *Glamorgan*, a County class DLG was partially rearmed with Exocet antiship missiles in the 1970s. She survived a hit from an Exocet in the closing stages of the Falklands campaign in June 1982.

class. These 11,000-ton ships appear underarmed for their size, with only two twin Standard (MR) missile-launchers and two lightweight 5-inch guns but they are formidable fighting ships, well equipped with sensors and data handling. The Mk 26 missile launchers can fire more rapidly than older launchers.

The Combat Information Centre (CIC) of a typical surface warfare combatant is located in the forward superstructure, just behind the bridge. In the *Belknap* class, for example, it is a vast area divided into spaces for the different functions. The central section of the CIC forms the command area, with positions for the Commanding Officer or Tactical Weapons Officer, the Ship's Weapons Coordinator (SWC) and the Surface/Subsurface Coordinator (SSSC).

In addition to the Standard missiles the SWC has responsibility for the eight Harpoon missiles. As they are a recent addition an extra console has been added to the left of the SWC console. Positions and tracks of friendly and hostile units are monitored on 'table-top' displays and vertical screens. Close to the command space, at the forward end of the CIC, is a 'flag space' where an admiral and his staff (if embarked) can follow progress of the battle on their own horizontal and vertical displays.

The SSSC supervises the ASW operations, isolated as much as possible from noise to allow the sonar operators to concentrate on the difficult task of following a contact. Alongside the Anti Submarine Warfare Officer (ASWO) supervises the hunting of underwater contacts. On his left, the Anti Submarine Air Controller (ASAC) directs the ship's helicopter toward a contact to allow it to drop depth charges or homing torpedoes.

The air-intercept and air-engagement consoles are located on the right hand side of the CIC. From a group of three the Fire Control System Coordinator (FCSC) and the Engagement Controller can direct the fire of the Mk 10 missile-launcher and the 5-inch gun.

The next generation of control systems makes current systems look very simple and old fashioned. The Aegis Fleet Defense System is designed to protect surface combatants, particularly the carriers, from the saturation attacks favored by the Russians. As far back as 1958 work had started on the ill-fated Typhon system; this was canceled but out of it came a study for an Advanced Surface Missile System (ASMS), later named Aegis after the shield of Zeus. At the heart of Aegis is a unique hexagonal planar (flat) radar array, the SPY-1A, which contains more than 4000 radiating elements. Instead of a rotating antenna, SPY-1A's four plane faces at the corners of the superstructure provide all-round and azimuth radar cover around the ship. The four electronically scanning arrays provide data to a bank of computers which automatically grade incoming threats in order of priority and provide fire control data. Air targets

539

are engaged by Standard SM-2 missiles, and the rapid fire Mk 26 launchers put a number of missiles into the air to provide rounds for the Aegis system to allocate as it chooses. As many as 18 Standard missiles can be tracked in the air, allowing the four SPG-62 illuminating radars to illuminate each target in turn and direct the missiles to the point where their own tracker head can home them to impact. By comparison a conventional 'double-ended' CG or CGN can engage four targets simultaneously, using the SM-1 missile.

There were long arguments about platforms for Aegis, but finally approval was given to modify the hull of the new *Spruance* class destroyer to accommodate Aegis. This resulted in the *DDG.47* design, later redesignated *CG.47* in recognition of the vastly improved performance of Aegis. The lead ship, named *Ticonderoga*, went to sea in May 1982 and joined the Atlantic Fleet in January 1983. More of the class are under construction, and by the early 1990s it will be unusual for a carrier battle group to be unaccompanied by at least one of these ships.

Like all high technology the cost of Aegis has delayed its introduction into service, but now that the development phase is over, cost and complexity of manufacture are coming down. A lighter and more compact form of SPY-1A will be installed in the new *Arleigh Burke* (DDG.51) class destroyers and four improved *Virginia* class nuclear cruisers (CGN.42-46) were planned to receive Aegis as well.

The US Navy is also modernizing its armory of antiship weapons. Although it was originally hoped that area defense SAMs like Tartar and Standard would have a limited surface capability this flexibility has always been suspect. After the Soviet SS-N-2 Styx missile had shown its deadliness by sinking the Israeli destroyer *Eilat* in 1967 the US Navy released funds for the development of a 60-mile range antiship missile. The Harpoon has been in service since the early 1970s, and exists in ship-launched, submarine-launched and air-launched variants. It is also widely deployed among friendly navies. The normal mode of deployment is in tubular canisters on deck, but in older destroyers it can also be launched from Asroc and Standard missile launchers, to allow existing magazines to be used.

Harpoon follows a preset flight path under inertial guidance, and when it is close to the target it switches on its radar seeker and executes a 'pop up' maneuver to allow it to dive onto the target for maximum destructive effect. Later Harpoons have been modified to allow the missile to follow a 'sea-skimming' path, making them much harder to detect.

Above left: The Soviet Kara class antisubmarine cruisers are successors to the Kresta IIs but with gas turbine propulsion. Left: Although once denounced by Krushchev as useless, several of the elderly *Sverdlov* class cruisers remain in service as command ships.

Other navies have adopted antiship missiles to counter the threat from the Soviet Styx. France developed its MM-38 Exocet, but unlike the Harpoon, the designers made it a sea-skimmer right from the start. Like Harpoon it is a 'fire and forget' weapon which needs only initial identification and fixing of the target before being launched, but the MM-38 version has only horizon range. Later variants include the longer-range MM-40, the air-launched AM-39 and the submarine-launched SM-39. Italy produced the Otomat, a much larger missile using an air breathing engine to gain longer range, and it has been sold widely. Israel became the first Western navy to fire antiship missiles in anger when in 1973 its fast missile boats won a convincing victory with its home developed Gabriel missiles over Styx-equipped Syrian and Egyptian FPBs. The Norwegians also developed a small missile, the Penguin, to take advantage of the numerous islands and fjords along their coast. Unlike the others it homes on infrared emissions from the target. This allows the use of passive sensors, making the launching patrol boat harder to detect.

Although cruise missiles are not new (the German V1 was nothing more than a strategic cruise missile, and several derivatives were operational in the 1950s) new technology has made them more reliable and accurate. The new BGM-109 Tomahawk is the naval cruise missile, and it exists in two versions, a 350-mile tactical missile, and a 1600-mile strategic missile. The heart of the Tomahawk and its land- and air-launched equivalents is a Terrain Contour Matching Radar (TERCOM) which forms part of TAINS (Tercom-Aided Inertial Navigation System). In simple terms, TAINS allows the missile to fly at 15–100 meters' height, following ground contours by comparing them with a 'radar map' stored in the computer memory.

From the Navy's point of view Tomahawk has the advantage of flexibility, as it can be used to attack surface ships or to threaten important land targets as part of the nuclear deterrent. This means, for example, that nuclear attack submarines and surface warships can be armed with both types of weapon, whereas a Trident or Poseidon submarine has only one function. Opponents of cruise missiles say that they 'lower the nuclear threshold' by blurring the distinction between strategic deterrent forces and tactical forces, but there is no doubt that the cruise missile offers enormous tactical advantages to the US Navy, and it is easy to understand why the Soviet Union wishes to limit their deployment.

To exploit the potential of the Tomahawk missile the US Navy plans to build up four Surface Action Groups (SAGs) based on the four *Iowa* class battleships. The *New Jersey* (BB.62) saw action in Vietnam in 1966–69, then joined her sisters *Iowa* (BB.61), *Missouri* (BB.63) and *Wisconsin* (BB.64) in mothballs and is now at sea again. Under President Reagan's plans to expand the US Navy, plans were announced

P73

Above: The F-14 Tomcat is the standard US Navy carrier interceptor aircraft. The Tomcat shown is armed with Phoenix missiles capable of destroying targets at 60 miles range.
Left: The French patrol boat *La Combattante* was used to test the Exocet antiship missile.
Below: FRS.1 Sea Harriers seen in the light gray camouflage scheme introduced shortly before the Falklands campaign.

to recommission all four and to rearm them with a mix of Harpoons and Tomahawks, as the core element of the new SAGs. The rationale is that four large missile platforms will pose such a potent threat to the Soviet Navy that significant forces will have to be allocated to defend against them, thereby tying down forces that would otherwise be free to operate offensively against US and allied forces. The four battleships have not seen much service, and so despite being 40 years old are in good condition; to build new hulls would cost billions of dollars and would take at least five years.

The SAGs have been criticized on the grounds that they would be excessively vulnerable, but the US Navy points out that modern electronic aids and close-in weapons can be mounted in profusion on such large hulls. The SAGs would be protected by the Carrier Battle Groups, and in any case the sheer size of the 48,000-ton hulls gives them the power to absorb a number of missile hits. The *New Jersey* recommissioned in December 1982 with an interim armament of 32 Harpoon missiles in quadruple canisters, and a defensive armament of six 20mm Phalanx 'Gatlings' added. The *Iowa* is receiving a more elaborate conversion, with Tomahawk missiles in armored box launchers, and after she is complete in 1983 the *Missouri* and *Wisconsin* will follow; after that the *New Jersey* will be brought up to a similar standard. If funds are available it is even hoped to give the battleships a limited air capability, with helicopters or even AV-8 Harrier V/STOL aircraft operating from a flight deck aft, but the cost of removing a triple 16-inch gun turret makes such a conversion extremely expensive.

Tomahawk missiles will, of course, arm smaller surface combatants. The new *Arleigh Burke* class (DDG.51) destroyers will carry a total of 90 missiles in vertical launchers, including SM-2 SAMs, Tomahawks and Asroc ASW missiles. What is certain is that after years of neglect surface warfare is once again a primary naval task, for it has at last been recognized that if ships cannot safely cross the water, control of that sea has been lost.

So far we have looked only at major combatants, but there is a whole field of surface warfare in which major warships play little or no part. The defense of coastal waters is entrusted to small strike craft, sometimes called FACs or Fast Attack Craft. They are the lineal descendants of the *Schnellboote*, R-Boats, MTBs, MGBs and PT-Boats which fought so many desperate actions in World War II, but modern technology has given them much greater punch.

Whereas most Western navies had run down their light forces after World War II the Soviet Navy kept large numbers of strike craft in commission, mainly with the intention of frustrating what they imagined to be the Western aim of invading the Russian landmass. Under Stalin the Navy was entrusted with protecting Mother Russia's flanks, and from 1952

some 500 P-4 and P-6 type motor torpedo boats were built. In 1959–61 a number of P-6 hulls were converted to launch the SS-N-2 Styx surface-to-surface missile.

These Komar type boats were tiny, only 85ft long, but their two missiles had a range of about 25 miles. The Komar was only an interim conversion, and shortly afterward a proper missile boat, the Osa type appeared. The hull was 131ft long, allowing four Styx missiles as well as twin 30mm guns and fire control and search radars to be fitted.

The Western world made no attempt to copy the Komar and Osa, apart from fitting some fast patrol boats with SS-11 short range wire-guided missiles, and indeed largely ignored the large number of missile boats transferred to pro-Soviet nations, until 21 October 1967, that is, when they suddenly leapt into prominence.

The event which transformed naval warfare was the sinking of the Israeli destroyer *Eilat* off Port Said by a pair of Komars lying behind the breakwater. No matter that the *Eilat* was 20 years old and lacked any modern defenses, or that she had been maintaining a fixed patrol line for days, inviting some sort of counterstroke from the Egyptians. What mattered was that two 75-ton boats had sunk a 1700-ton destroyer, with three out of four missiles.

What can only be described as a 'Styx Panic' swept through Western navies, and no fewer than five missile-programs received their first impetus from the *Eilat* sinking. The US Navy went ahead with its Harpoon program, the French immediately funded

Top: The *Philips van Almonde*, one of ten *Kortenaer* class frigates built for the Royal Netherlands Navy. Their main role is antisubmarine escort but they also carry a powerful antiship armament of eight Harpoon missiles.
Above: A Soviet Krivak class frigate refueling from an oil tanker. This is one of the 20 Krivak I type with twin 76mm guns.
Top left: A Jianghu class frigate and a Luda class DDG (right) of the Chinese PLA Navy at Woosung near Shanghai. The PLA Navy remains a coastal defense force for the moment but there are signs that larger ships are planned.

the MM-38 Exocet and the Italians started work in conjunction with the French on Otomat. Not surprisingly, the Israelis speeded up their own program, called Gabriel, and a not dissimilar weapon called Penguin went forward in Norway. The Royal Swedish Navy already possessed an antiship missile of its own, the Rb05, but this was not regarded as an unqualified success, and it was never seen as a serious competitor for the other weapons.

The Royal Navy, needing a weapon quickly, signified its intention to buy Exocet as soon as it was seen to be progressing well, and by 1974 the first British warship, the DLG *Norfolk* was carrying out firing trials in the Mediterranean. The adoption of Exocet by a leading NATO navy improved its chances, and the Federal German Navy also chose to instal it in a new type of fast patrol boat. This was the French *Combattante II* design, actually a French 47-meter modification of a German 45-meter design (a ruse to allow Germany to sell FPBs to Israel without ruffling Arab feelings). No fewer than 20 *Combattantes* were built for the Federal German Navy, which wished to use them to block the exit from the Baltic, using the small islands off Denmark as cover.

As part of NATO's strategic objective of bottling up the Soviet Baltic Fleet in time of war, the Royal Danish Navy was also encouraged to build strike

Composition of a Typical Carrier Air Group

Two interceptor squadrons, each with F-14 Tomcats	24 aircraft
Three attack squadrons, each with A-7 Corsairs or A-6 Intruders	36 aircraft
One recce detachment, with RF-14 Tomcats	3 aircraft
One AEW detachment, with E-2 Hawkeyes	4 aircraft
One ECM squadron, with EA-6 Prowlers	4 aircraft
One tanker detachment, with KA-6 Intruders	4 aircraft
Two ASW squadrons, one with S-3 Vikings, one with SH-3 Sea King helicopters	10 aircraft 6 helicopters
Total	91 aircraft

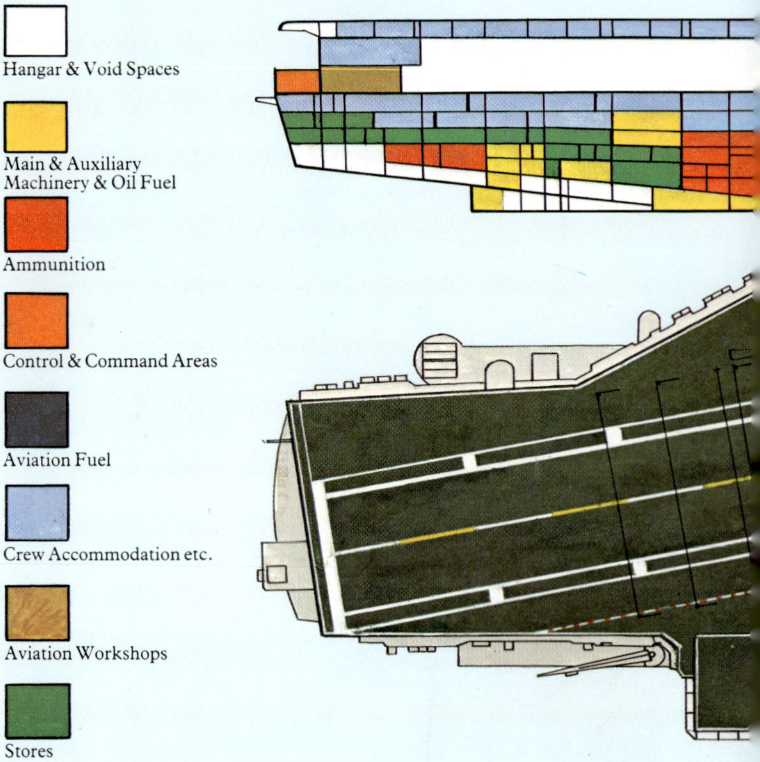

Below: The *Forrestal* class carrier *Ranger* makes a high-speed turn.
Bottom right: An A-7E Corsair II attack aircraft in flight over the *Kitty Hawk* class carrier *America*.

Diagrams showing the internal and flight deck arrangements on the *Forrestal*. The *Forrestals'* successors have had the port side aircraft elevator moved to the after end of the flight deck to improve operating efficiency.

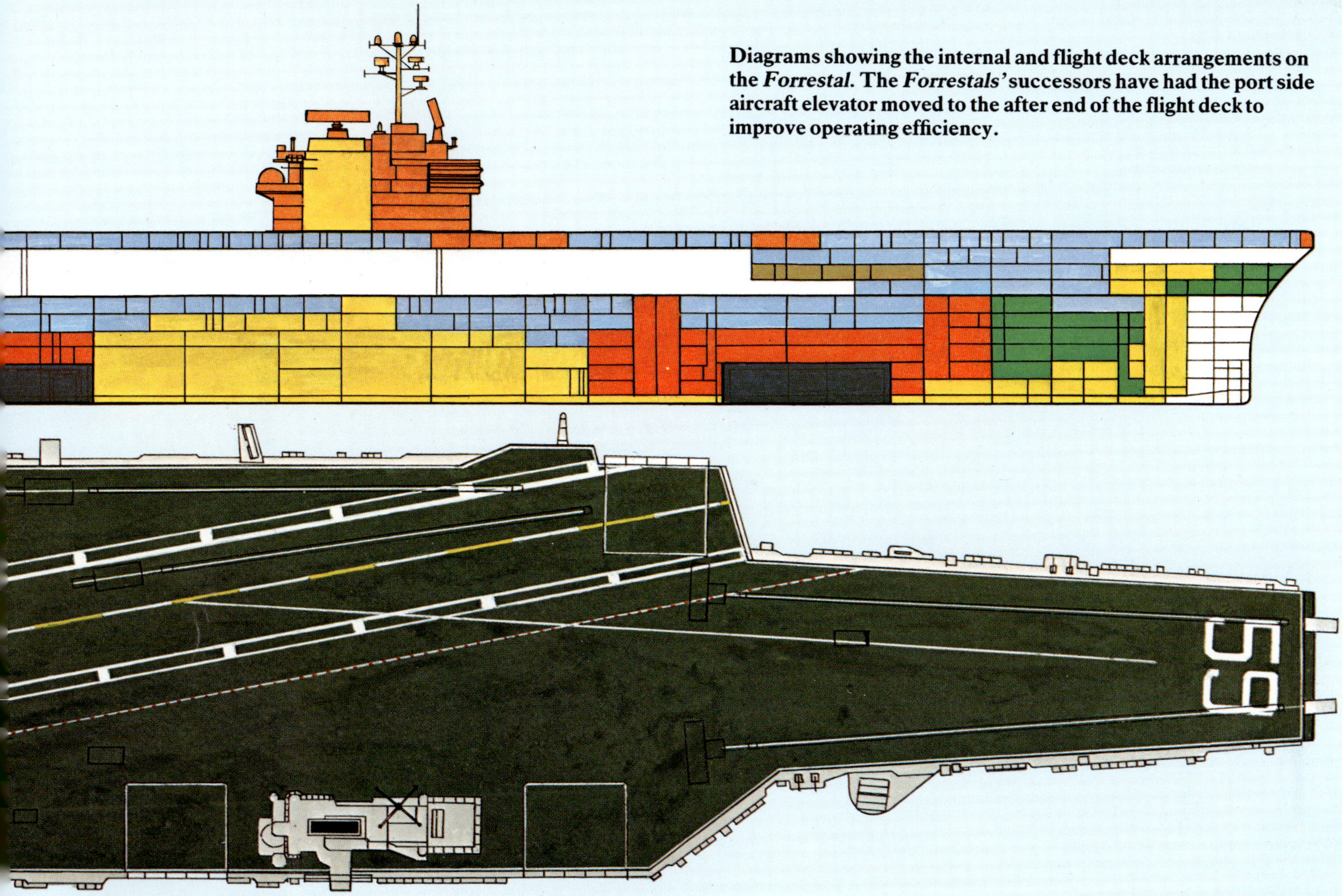

craft, but the Danes turned to Sweden for technical assistance. The Swedes have a large archipelago of literally hundreds of islands, an ideal hunting ground for small craft, and like other Scandinavian countries had enthusiastically adopted the torpedo 80 years earlier. With help from the German Lürssen firm the Swedish Navy developed the 160-ton *Spica* type of torpedo boat, armed with six wire-guided torpedoes and a rapid-firing 57mm gun and driven at 38 knots by triple gas turbines. It was this design which the Danes took as the basis for their *Willemoes* class, but they substituted an Italian 76mm gun for the Swedish Bofors 57mm gun.

The Norwegians went their own way, developing a series of smaller craft to fire Penguin. This small missile relies on infrared homing, as against the active radar seeker in Exocet and other missiles, as the Royal Norwegian Navy's requirement was for a system which did not give away the firing craft's position. Thus the Penguin-armed craft rely heavily on opto-electronic (optronic) sensors to detect their targets. A remarkable feature of Penguin when it appeared was its ability to make a 'dog-leg' maneuver in flight; it allows a missile, for example, to fly around an island behind which the target may be sheltering. Today the air-launched version of Penguin is in service, and Penguins have been fitted to larger warships.

Only the Israeli and Russian-designed missile boats have been tested in action, and the results give some idea of what future battles will be like. The tactics needed to defeat the Soviet SS-N-2 Styx missile were complicated by the fact that the Gabriel Mk 1 had a range of 21,000 meters, as against 40–50,000 meters for the Styx. The solution devised by the Israelis was to use evasive maneuvering and electronic warfare (jamming, decoys and analysis of radar and radio signals) to get their missile boats within range without being hit. We may never know the full story but we can judge how effective the Israeli plans were by the fact that 13 *Reshef* and *Sa'ar* class boats, mounting between them 63 Gabriels, suffered no losses in defeating 27 Syrian and Egyptian

Osa and Komar craft, mounting between them 85 Styxes of roughly twice the range.

Two battles took place, one off Latakia on the night of 6 October 1973 and the other on 8 October off Damietta, far to the south, off the Egyptian coast. In the Latakia battle a combat group of five Israeli missile boats ran into a group of Syrian patrol craft; while engaging them six Styx missiles were detected on radar. The Israeli boats dodged the missiles, but eight minutes later a second salvo of six missiles was detected. One was destroyed by fire from 76mm guns, and the other five passed harmlessly overhead.

Within a few minutes the range was down to 20,000 meters, and the Israeli boats were within Gabriel range. Two targets, reported to be Syrian missile boats, blew up, and about 20 minutes later a damaged Komar was sunk by 40mm Bofors guns. The outer screen of light craft was also dealt with, and the night's casualties included a minesweeper and a torpedo boat.

The battle of Damietta involved another combat group of five, which sighted four Osa boats at about 48,000 meters. A salvo of three missiles was detected, followed by three more, but each time the Israeli boats dodged them, making a total of 12 missiles which did not achieve a lock-on. Once again the Israelis closed the range, with disastrous results to the enemy. Two *Osas* were seen to blow up, and a third ran aground, to be destroyed by gunfire.

What Israeli reports do not make clear is exactly *how* the missiles were decoyed. It is claimed in some quarters that in both battles the combat groups were accompanied by helicopters flying overhead keeping tight formation. As soon as the Styx missiles were detected the helicopters dropped chaff to confuse the radar-seekers, and broke formation upward and outward. The effect of this stratagem would be to give the missile's radar seeker a 'picture' of a target which suddenly seemed to get larger and lift above the surface, which would explain why so many missiles flew overhead.

Partly as a result of these actions but also because

The newly-commissioned support carrier HMS *Illustrious* leaves for the Falklands on 2 August 1982. She relieved her sister *Invincible* and took over part of her air group. Note the Phalanx gun system fitted on the starboard stern corner of the flight deck.

Main picture: The nuclear carrier USS *Enterprise* (CVN.65) off San Diego. When built she was the world's largest warship and has recently been modernized with new radars as shown here.
Left: Radar operator at one of the displays in the CIC aboard the USS *Enterprise*.
Right: Although generally similar to the *Enterprise*, the *Nimitz* (CVN.68) and her sisters have only two reactors, instead of eight, and a number of other internal improvements.

47
49
35
46

Above left: Yak-36 Forger VTOL aircraft on the flight deck of the Soviet cruiser-carrier *Minsk*.
Above: The French helicopter cruiser *Jeanne d'Arc* is a training ship in peacetime but would become a helicopter carrier and command ship in wartime.
Left: The *Kiev* was the first of a class of four ships originally thought to be attack carriers but Western observers now assess them as hybrids, with cruiser armament, antisubmarine helicopters and a small group of Forgers for the strike role.

the small missile boat seems a better investment for a small navy, the building of missile boats has steadily increased. The Russians have put missiles into hydrofoils, and have steadily developed designs. NATO tried to get a similar trend under way, with plans for the United States, Italy and West Germany to collaborate in a NATO Hydrofoil program, but it failed when costs ran out of control. The Americans were left to go it alone with a planned class of six Patrol Missile Hydrofoils or PHMs, and after many changes of heart the PHM Squadron is now in operation at Key West, Florida. PHMRON Two, comprising the *Pegasus* (PHM.1), *Hercules* (PHM.2), *Taurus* (PHM. 3), *Aquila* (PHM.4), *Aries* (PHM.5) and *Gemini* (PHM.6), reached full strength at the end of 1982. The armament of each PHM is eight Harpoon antiship missiles in canisters aft, and a 76mm rapid-firing gun forward, giving them a remarkable punch for a craft only 147ft long and displacing only 231 tons. The single gas turbine drives two waterjet units on the after foils, and when speed rises above 12 knots the hydrofoil rises on its struts. With hull drag eliminated, speed then rises to over 40 knots.

Although the Italian Navy dropped out of the NATO Hydrofoil venture there was still great enthusiasm for the new technology. A smaller, cheaper Boeing prototype hydrofoil called *Tucumcari* was chosen as the basis, rather than the US Navy's PHM, and out of this came the *Sparviero*, 22.95 meters long and displacing only 64.5 tons. Like the *Pegasus* she is armed with a 76mm gun forward, but aft she has only two Otomat missiles. The *Sparviero* proved a great success and six more have been built, the *Nibbio* class. The only other armed hydrofoils in the West are the Israeli *Shimrit* class, which came into service in 1981–82. These two craft were built to a Grumman design, one in Florida and the second at Haifa. They are 70-tonners armed with a twin 30mm antiaircraft gun forward, two Gabriel missiles amidships and four Harpoon missiles aft. A feature of the design is a huge pineapple-shaped structure above the wheelhouse, believed to contain not only an optical fire control director but elaborate radar and signal intercept equipment. The Royal Navy operated a small hydrofoil in the fishery protection role for a while but found it unsuited to their needs, and she was put up for sale in 1982.

The Western world looks to the Israelis as acknowledged experts in the design and operation of strike

9
MARINE

Above: The carrier *Nimitz* seen while taking on ammunition from a store ship. Large carriers need to replenish aircraft fuel and ordnance frequently during intensive flying operations.
Left: A Super Etendard, the French Navy's standard strike aircraft, on the catapult of a French carrier.

craft, so it is worthwhile looking at their latest fast patrol boat. The 500-ton *Aliyah* class have grown to 61.7 meters in length and are armed with eight Harpoon missiles, four Gabriels, a single 40mm gun, a new design of twin 30mm AA gun and a twin 20mm as well as four machine guns. But they also find space for a hangar and flight deck to operate a Bell Kiowa helicopter. Apart from providing valuable reconnaissance the helicopter can also provide over-the-horizon data to permit the Harpoon missiles to exploit their full 60-mile range. However the provision of a helicopter on such a small hull may prove too ambitious and there are reports that the rest of the class will have a 76mm gun and four more Gabriels instead of the hangar and flight deck. However, the *Aliyah* class demonstrate the trend for strike craft to cope with the problem of providing better command and control, as the range of weapons gets greater.

Nothing has been said so far about the Chinese Navy. More correctly designated the People's Liberation Army (PLA) Navy, it is still a force largely dedicated to surface warfare. Like the Soviet Navy of the 1950s and early 1960s its main role is to defend mainland China against invasion, and has little or no preoccupation with power-projection at any distance from the home base.

Notwithstanding its modest aims, the most impressive feature of the PLA Navy is its sheer size. At the beginning of 1982 the strength stood at 100 submarines, 11 destroyers, 22 frigates, some 200 missile boats, nearly 300 torpedo boats, nearly 1000 patrol craft and minesweepers, and 500 amphibious warfare craft. Many of these are either Russian-built or based on Soviet technology, but since the breach with the

Below: The French carrier *Foch* refueling the destroyer *Suffren*. *Foch* and her sister *Clemenceau* are to be replaced by nuclear carriers in the late 1980s.
Inset, right: The conventional carrier *John F. Kennedy* and her three sisters are improved versions of the original *Forrestal* class 'super carriers' built in the late 1950s.
Below right: The primary role for HMS *Invincible* and her two sisters is to give air cover to antisubmarine operations and deploy large ASW helicopters in mid ocean.

Soviet Union efforts have been made to develop indigenous designs and weapons. Despite this understandable desire for self-reliance the Chinese make no secret of their wish to import Western technology for the modernization of their navy, and it remains to be seen what equipment will be bought.

The main strength of the surface fleet comprises a class of destroyers known as the Luda class, because they were built at the Luda Shipyard in Manchuria. Although based on the Soviet Kotlin design they differ in several respects. Amidships they have two sets of triple antiship missiles; the missile is reported to be a development of the SS-N-2 Styx. The defensive armament includes two twin 130mm dual-purpose gun mountings, two quadruple 57mm gun mountings and two twin 25mm. The ships are still under construction, and at least 14 hulls are known to exist.

It will be obvious that the Luda class lack any sort of defense against modern aircraft, and clearly it is a matter of priority to remedy this deficiency. A proposal was made by a British consortium to reequip at least two out of nine Ludas with the GWS.30 Sea Dart surface-to-air missile, as well as new radars and electronics. No details were published, and the contract has since been deferred because of financial and political decisions, but the broad details can be deduced. The Sea Dart system would probably have been sited aft, in place of the twin 130mm guns; a forward position would have been exposed to spray and the hull might not have been wide enough to accommodate the magazine. New superstructures and bridgework would have been needed to accommodate the electronics, and the present low, raked funnels would have had to be raised to clear the tracker radars. The air-warning radar would probably have been the Marconi Type 1022, and it seems likely that Sea Dart would have been controlled by Marconi ST810SD trackers rather than the bulky Type 909 system. The forward twin 130mm gun mounting

HMS *Hermes*, flagship of the Falklands Task Force, seen on her return to Portsmouth on 21 July 1982. She was converted from a conventional carrier by the addition of a prominent ski-jump for launching Sea Harriers but retains a capability as an amphibious assault ship.

would probably have been retained for shore bombardment, and the twin 57mm for close range anti-aircraft defense. The antisubmarine armament would have been replaced too, with new sonars and triple torpedo tubes.

The remainder of the destroyer force is made up of four Russian-built Gordy class, 1700-ton ships which have been rearmed with four SS-N-2C missiles. They are now over 40 years old, and it seems highly probable that they will be replaced when more Ludas are commissioned.

The next class of surface escorts is the modern Jianghu class, which are capable of $25\frac{1}{2}$ knots on a displacement of 1900 tons full load. The remaining armament is light; two single 100mm guns, four twin 37mm AA guns and two ASW rocket launchers. On the same hull, the Jiangdong class mount surface-to-air missiles, but reports from intelligence sources suggest that the system is not yet operational.

In 1954–57 four of the Soviet Riga class frigates or light escorts were built at Shanghai, followed by five similar Jiangnan class. The first four have been rearmed with missiles, a triple group of SS-N-2Cs on a rotating turntable, as in the Luda class, whereas the Jiangnan class have three 100mm guns of obsolete design, four twin 37mm AA guns and ASW rockets.

Apart from some very ancient veterans of World War II the remainder of the PLA Navy's surface strength is concentrated in strike craft and patrol boats. There are approximately a hundred locally-built versions of the Soviet Osa type, and a steel-hulled variant of the smaller Komar, known as the Hoku type.

Like their erstwhile Soviet allies the Chinese showed a keen interest in hydrofoils, and some of their numerous Huchuan type torpedo boats built in the late 1960s have been exported. There is also a hydrofoil version of the Hoku missile boat, known to Western Intelligence as the Homa. The remainder of the torpedo boat force is made up of Russian-built P.4 and P.6 types. The best-known local patrol craft are the Shanghai IIs, sturdy diesel-engined craft armed with two twin 37mm guns, machine guns and depth charges. In all as many as 350 of these craft may have been constructed, and they have been followed by the Hainan class, armed with 57mm guns.

The PLA Navy is known to be looking for ways to update its fast strike craft fleet. The only recent new design reported was the Hola type first seen in 1970, which was apparently an enlargement of the Osa design, but as only one was seen we must assume that she was not a success. Not long after that a very strange craft was photographed; she had no fewer than six unidentified missiles. Just what she was has never been discovered, but one suggestion is that she was simply a 'prop' for a film. For the present there are no further signs of any change in the PLA Navy's strength.

5. AIR DEFENSE

The guided missile cruiser (formerly destroyer leader) USS *Leahy* (CG.16) and her sisters were the first 'double ended' missile ships.

Ever since World War II, when Japanese torpedo- and dive-bombers devastated the US Pacific Fleet at Pearl Harbor and sank the British capital ships *Prince of Wales* and *Repulse* off Malaya, defense against the air threat has been paramount. The bloody operations off Okinawa added a new element, the suicide attack, in which a human brain functioned as a terminal guidance system to turn the aircraft into a missile, rather than a delivery vehicle.

The answer, as we have seen, was to design antiaircraft missiles which could be guided by radar to the point of impact. In theory at least, such missiles could guarantee the destruction of an attacking aircraft, whereas gunfire, even with proximity-fuzed shells, could only predict a percentage of hits in the area of the aircraft.

The first missiles were bulky, and so cruisers had to be converted to accommodate the tracker radars and the magazines. In all 11 US Navy cruisers were converted to act as antiaircraft screening ships for the fast carrier task forces, and the nuclear *Long Beach* was built for the same purpose. However by the 1960s it was clear that smaller destroyer-sized hulls could accommodate the same type of firepower, even if they lacked the same magazine stowage and could not accommodate an admiral and his staff.

The first missile-armed fleet escorts designed for the task were planned as 'frigates' or Destroyer Leaders (DLGs). The *Farragut* (DLG.6) class was the result of recommendations made by the Schindler Committee as long ago as 1954, making the case for specialized Fast Task Force Escorts equipped for Anti Aircraft Warfare (AAW). The initial design substituted a twin launcher for Terrier missiles in place of two single 5inch guns aft. After some hesitation all ten ships of the program (DLG.6-15) were built with missiles, but in response to the growing threat from submarines the antisubmarine armament was strengthened.

The Terrier missile had started life as a supersonic test vehicle for the long range Talos missile, but preceded it into service as work was accelerated by the outbreak of the Korean War in 1950. Like other missiles of that era it was something of a disappointment, being difficult to maintain and erratic in performance. Although Operational Evaluation (OPEVAL) did not begin until 1955, a Terrier Improvement Program had already been running for two years. The method of guidance was changed from beam-riding to semiactive homing, and the original range of 10 miles was doubled, and then redoubled by 1964 to 40 miles. Today it is no longer in production, but Terrier-armed ships are being rearmed with the Standard (Extended Range) RIM-67A, which has a similar airframe but new electronics.

At 4167 tons (light) the *Farraguts* were big and costly, and there was clearly a need for a smaller destroyer (DDG) for fleet screening. The solution was to design a single-stage version of the Terrier which could go into a 3000-ton or smaller ship. Tartar was intended to be effective between 2000 and 15,000 yards and at an altitude of 50,000 feet. Subsequently these figures were raised to 25,000 yards and 65,000 feet respectively, and development was advanced as rapidly as possible. Unfortunately the weapon system did not live up to its early promise, and when OPEVAL began in the *Charles F Adams* (DDG.2) in 1961 there were many red faces. Maintenance problems, particularly in the fire control system, proved almost insurmountable and OPEVAL had to be terminated in November 1961 without the system being passed as serviceable.

Despite these disappointments the Tartar-armed destroyers of the *Charles F Adams* class were successful. In all 23 ships were commissioned between 1960 and 1964, and they are still highly regarded; three were built for the Federal German Navy (the *Lütjens* class) and three for the Royal Australian Navy (the *Perth* class). From the *Berkeley* (DDG.15) onward the twin-arm launcher was replaced by the single-arm Mk 13, which was more reliable and capable of firing the same number of missiles. The later ships (DDG. 15-24) have undergone an AAW modernization since 1981; this involves replacing Tartar with the Standard (Medium Range) RIM-66A and improved electronics.

By the late 1950s the missile was taking over completely from the gun in air defense, and the successors to the *Farragut* class, the nine *Leahy* (DLG.16) class marked a new departure. They were made 'double-ended', with twin Terrier launchers forward and aft. Instead of the conventional profile of the *Farraguts* they were given two 'macks' or combined mast/stacks to save deck space. Each twin-arm launcher is served by a 40-round magazine and two large AN/SPG-55 trackers. At 5146 tons (light) they were another 1000 tons bigger than the previous DLGs, and the three-quarter length forecastle deck enhanced their appearance.

The size and cost of the *Leahy* class horrified Congress, and there was pressure on the US Navy to build a successor to the *Charles F Adams* class, but more austere. Even by cutting the number of missiles to 12, the requirement to push endurance up by 1500 miles to 6000nm and the inclusion of the new AN/SQS-26 sonar resulted in a ship which was far more expensive than the *Adams* class. Then the planners decided that Terrier was a better missile for a large ship, and to save further trouble the hull of the *Leahy* was adapted. The nine *Belknap* (DLG.26) class were built in 1964–67, and they have been followed by two nuclear equivalents, the *Bainbridge* (DLGN.25) and *Truxtun* (DLGN.35), and the *California* and *Virginia* class nuclear cruisers.

Other navies wanted to build missile ships to protect their major fleet units against air attack. The British started development of a beam-riding missile

The Italian cruiser *Vittorio Veneto* has a twin Terrier/Asroc missile system forward and a large helicopter hangar and flight deck aft. She normally operates four AB.202 antisubmarine helicopters.

Above: The USS *Horne* (CG.30), a unit of the *Belknap* class.
Above left: The USS *Cochrane* and the rest of the *Charles F. Adams* class are the mainstay of US fleet air defense forces.
Below left: The new Aegis missile cruiser *Ticonderoga*.

immediately after the war, and the Staff Requirement was issued in 1946. The first test vehicle flew five years later, enabling the dimensions of the airframe to be fixed. Unfortunately large booster rockets could not be manufactured in Britain at the time, and so four $\frac{1}{4}$-ton boosters were adopted, wrapped around the body of the missile. This resulted in a very bulky missile known as Seaslug, which in turn had a serious impact on the design of the ships which were to use them. Thus, instead of the vertical loading system used in the first Terrier-armed cruisers, the County class DLGs had a huge tunnel through the superstructure. The missiles travel from the forward magazine back through the ship, having the wings put on, circuits checked etc, before being run out on the launcher.

Two Seaslug ships took part in the fighting around the Falklands in 1982, and although the beam-riding guidance system is not suited to attacking modern high speed aircraft HMS *Antrim* was able to break up formations of Mirages by firing Seaslug as a barrage weapon, using a simple alteration to the fuzing to give a time-delay burst. Her sister *Glamorgan* put Seaslug to an even less orthodox purpose by firing it at Argentine artillery positions. It was reasoned that, as the missiles are to be withdrawn for scrapping, they should at least be fired to destruction if the opportunity arose. In fact the scrap value of guided missiles being negligible the normal method of disposal is to fire them live during exercises. Old missiles can also be used as target vehicles for more modern missiles.

The eight County class DLGs were completed in 1962–70. In the year that the first ship commissioned work started on a missile to follow the Seaslug. Named Sea Dart, it was driven by a ramjet and used semi-active homing. Its effective range is about 25 miles, and one of its advantages is good performance against low-level targets. During the Falklands fighting the DDG *Exeter* shot down two Argentine A-4 Skyhawks in quick succession, and is credited with a 'kill' at 50 feet.

The first ships designed for Sea Dart were a quartet of DLGs intended to screen a pair of aircraft carriers planned in 1966. In the event the carriers were canceled and only one of the DLGs, HMS *Bristol* was built. A class of small DDGs was started in 1970, the *Sheffield* class, but on 3500 tons they proved too small, and the design had to be stretched by adding 30ft more. The ten *Sheffield* class (Type 42) and the four stretched *Manchester* class were designed without allowance for a close range defensive armament, although after the sinking of HMS *Sheffield* by an air-launched Exocet missile and the loss of her sister *Coventry* to a conventional glide-bombing attack by A-4 Skyhawks the rest of the class were hurriedly given twin 30mm guns amidships as a close range defense.

The *Sheffield* was in fact sunk by a combination of human errors. Hostile air activity had been reported but the ship was not brought to Action Stations, and the main radar was closed down to permit a message to be transmitted via the satellite link. The Exocet was launched from one of a pair of Super Etendards some 25 miles away, and was apparently undetected, although it seems likely that an electronic warning was received but ignored. The missile struck on the starboard side, above the waterline and went through both engine rooms before hitting the after engine room bulkhead without exploding. Even so the friction of the missile body and unspent fuel in the rocket motor was sufficient to set the fuel alight, and within seconds the central part of the ship was filled with choking black smoke. Even though damage control parties were able to get power supplies working, smoke made it impossible for firefighters to reach the flames, and after five hours the ship was abandoned after the crew had been taken off. Six days later the gutted hulk was cut loose and allowed to sink in deep water.

The *Coventry*, in contrast, achieved considerable success, lying to the north of Falkland Sound in company with the frigate *Broadsword*, tracking hostile aircraft on her long range air surveillance radar, and directing Sea Harrier aircraft to attack them. In fact she had been performing that task from 1 May, the day in which the Task Force entered the Total Exclusion Zone around the Falklands.

On the first day the air battle went well, with seven Argentinian aircraft shot down by the Sea Harriers of the carriers *Invincible* and *Hermes*. The first engagement with Sea Dart took place when *Coventry* fired a single Sea Dart to destroy two Skyhawks at a range of 25 miles, and a few hours later a second missile destroyed a troop-carrying helicopter at 13 miles' range. On 24 May the *Coventry*'s coordination of air defense off Falkland Sound vectored the Sea Harriers onto three 'kills', and the following day she shot down three aircraft with missiles. But at about 6 pm four aircraft made a determined low-level attack. The frigate *Broadsword*, following astern, was about to fire Sea Wolf short range missiles at the attackers when the *Coventry* swung across her bows while taking avoiding action, and in the confusion a solitary Skyhawk was able to get through and hit with three out of four 1000 pound bombs.

Right: The Norwegian *Aegir* is a small coastal escort or corvette armed with a single 3-inch gun and ASW weapons
Below right: After carrying out the first sea trials of the Sea Wolf missile, the frigate HMS *Penelope* was modernized with four Exocet antiship missiles in place of her twin 4.5-inch gun.
Main picture: The Italian DDG *Ardito* has the US Standard missile system and associated radars aft but the rest of her armament is of Italian design comprising two 5-inch guns, four 3-inch guns and six antisubmarine torpedo tubes

Main picture: The nuclear powered guided missile cruiser USS *Truxtun* (CGN.35) like her predecessor the *Bainbridge* was designed to screen nuclear-powered aircraft carriers.
Left: The nuclear missile cruiser *Arkansas* (CGN.41) is the last of a series of six fast carrier escorts. Experience has shown that the nuclear carriers do indeed need escorts with equally high endurance.

Those in the *Coventry*'s Operations Room remembered only a flash of searing flame, followed by dense clouds of black smoke. Those who were still alive were badly burned, and even their clothing was alight. All power and communications were destroyed and the ship began to list to port. Within 15 minutes she was lying on her side, and then she slowly rolled over. Surprisingly, only 19 men were killed by the explosion, and some 280 officers and ratings escaped.

The Task Force had left Britain with only three air defense ships, and had now lost all three, for in addition to the *Sheffield* and *Coventry*, their sister *Glasgow* had been disabled by a bomb early in the fighting. Luckily reinforcements which had arrived a few days earlier included the DLG *Bristol* and the DDGs *Exeter* and *Cardiff*. The *Exeter* had a newer air warning radar than the earlier ships of the class, and as already mentioned, this helped her to achieve missile 'kills' against low flying aircraft. Her moment of fame came on 30 May, when the Super Etendards made an attempt to sink the carrier *Invincible*, using their last Exocet missile; two of the six accompanying Skyhawks were destroyed by Sea Dart missiles from the *Exeter*, persuading the survivors to head for home.

The most important lesson learned by the British in the air defense of the Task Force was that older surveillance radars were not good enough to cope with low level attacks. With no airborne early warning to guide defending Sea Harriers, all depended on the radars in the DDGs and the carriers, but the ships were not equipped with the sort of '3-D' radars which the US Navy insists on for its air defense ships. A three-dimensional radar is, in simple terms, one which combines a height-finding radar with the conventional type capable of giving range and bearing of targets. The objection to a 3-D radar is that height-finding is generally less accurate than the ranging and bearing indication, but this is comparatively unimportant, so long as the defending aircraft are correctly vectored to an altitude where their own radars can take over.

The Type 965 long range air warning radar was designed in the 1950s to track comparatively high flying Soviet bombers, and does not provide data at a fast enough rate to cope with fast targets. Even worse, it is intended to work with a target-indicating radar, the Type 992Q, which has difficulty in identifying targets against the 'clutter' of land or the surface of the sea. The need for a new Surveillance and Target-Indicating Radar (known as STIR for short) was recognized, and the Type 1022 fitted in the *Exeter* and later DDGs is regarded as an interim STIR. Ironically, a year before the Falklands, development of a new STIR radar had been canceled, but a new staff requirement has since been drawn up for a cheaper commercial equivalent.

The French Navy also decided to go its own way on missile development, but found the cost of developing area defense weapons a great strain on its resources. Even with American technical assistance the Masurca missile (roughly equivalent to the US Navy's Terrier) had a lengthy period of trials and development before it became operational. To gain practical experience the decision was taken to convert five large destroyers of the *Surcouf* class (T47 type) to DDGs, using American radars and missiles. Between 1962 and 1965 the *Dupetit-Thouars*, *Kersaint*, *Bouvet* and *du Chayla* were rebuilt with a single-arm Mk 13 launcher for Tartar missiles and two SPG-51 trackers in place of the after pair of 127mm gun mountings, and an SPS-39A '3-D' radar antenna on the mainmast.

The first Masurca-armed ships were the 'frigates' *Suffren* and *Duquesne*, built in 1962–70. When they first appeared they set new standards in appearance, with a single tall 'mack' amidships and a vast 'golf ball' dome protecting the big DRBI-23 surveillance radar. In the 1970s the armament was further increased by the addition of four MM-38 Exocet antiship missiles. In the interim Masurca underwent the same sort of updating as Terrier, being converted from beam-riding to semi-active homing.

Only one more ship was destined to receive Masurca. In 1970–72 the 8500-ton cruiser *Colbert* underwent a major reconstruction, during which her after 127mm and 57mm guns were replaced by a twin-arm launcher and two DRBR-51 trackers. When the time came to order an air-defense version of the new C70 type antisubmarine 'corvettes' or destroyers, the missile chosen was the American Standard SM-1 instead of the Masurca. The electronics, however, are French: a new DRBJ-11 phased-array radar and a SENIT 6 action-information system.

The Dutch and Italian Navies have been content to buy American missiles for installation in their own ships. The cruiser *de Zeven Provincien* was given a Terrier system aft, replacing two twin 6-inch gun turrets, while the large DDGs *Tromp* and *de Ruyter* completed in 1975–76 had Standard SM-1 systems. The last two of 14 'Standard' or *Kortenaer* class frigates built since 1975 are being built to a modified air-defense design, also with Standard SM-1 missiles.

Typically the Italians went for a most elaborate conversion of the old 6-inch gunned cruiser *Giuseppe Garibaldi*, dating from the 1930s. Between 1957 and 1962 she was completely gutted and rebuilt with a new bridge, upperworks and single funnel. The former 'A' and 'B' 6-inch guns were replaced by twin 135mm (5.3-inch) guns, eight 76mm guns were sited amidships, and a Terrier system was installed aft. There was talk at the time of creating a multinational NATO surface deterrent fleet, and to demonstrate its feasibility the *Garibaldi* was given four Polaris launch tubes below the quarterdeck. Test vehicles were fired from these tubes, but the idea of deploying Polaris in surface ships went out of fashion and the *Garibaldi* never embarked them operationally.

Below: Three modified versions of the *Charles F. Adams* class DDGs were built for the Federal German Navy in the 1970s as the *Lütjens* class. The *Molders* is shown here.
Bottom: The French DDG *Suffren* is armed with the French Masurca SAM aft, the Malafon antisubmarine missile amidships and 100mm guns forward.

Above: Sea Dart missiles, the standard British medium-range SAM, on the twin-arm launcher of the DDG HMS *Bristol*. Left: The Italian Otomat antiship missile being fired from a Venezuelan *Lupo* class frigate during trials off Sardinia.

In their next class of missile ships the Italian designers achieved a remarkable blend of air-defense and antisubmarine capabilities. A twin-arm Terrier launcher was installed forward, while the after part of the ship was devoted to a flight deck and hangar capable of housing three Sea King helicopters. The idea was overambitious, for on 5000 tons it proved impossible to carry the big helicopters, and four smaller types had to be embarked. The *Andrea Doria* and *Caio Duilio* pointed the way to other hybrid helicopter cruisers, but the next ship, the *Vittorio Veneto* was made considerably larger to improve the helicopter handling. She is much more successful in many ways, not least because the Terrier launcher was modified to permit Asroc antisubmarine missiles to be launched from the same magazines.

Only two more classes of air-defense ships have been built for the Italian Navy, but they are more conventional DDGs armed with Tartar SAMs, rather than hybrid helicopter-cruisers, the *Impavido*, *Intrepido*, *Audace* and *Ardito*.

The Japanese built their first missile-armed ship in 1962–65, the 3000-ton *Amatsukaze*. Unlike the European ships she was armed with Tartar missiles, but these have since been replaced by Standard SM-1. She has been followed by the three *Tachikaze* class, completed 1976–82, and a new class of gas turbine-driven DDGs is currently building. They will be armed with Standard SAMs and eight Harpoon missiles, as well as 5-inch guns, Asroc missiles and antisubmarine torpedoes. The unnamed *DDG.171* is also the first warship to be driven by the Rolls-Royce SM1A Spey gas turbine.

At this point it is time to turn to the Soviet Navy, for the Russians could hardly ignore the trend toward area-defense SAMs in Western ships, particularly as their surface warships could expect to be attacked by Western carrier aircraft. In 1961–62 two six year old Kotlin class destroyers were taken in hand for conversion to operate the SA-N-1 Goa, following trials with a land missile, codenamed Guideline, in the cruiser *Dzerzhinski*. Apparently the Guideline was unsuitable, for it very soon gave way to the Goa, which has since been installed in other classes.

In all eight Kotlin class destroyers were reconstructed as DDGs, starting with the *Bravy*. One, the *Spravedlivy*, was transferred to Poland in 1970 and renamed *Warszawa*. In 1963 the first of a new class codenamed Kashin appeared. She was the first major warship driven entirely by gas turbines and also the first Soviet purpose-built DDG, with twin-arm Goa launchers forward and aft, backed up by two twin 76mm dual-purpose gun mountings and a set of quintuple torpedo tubes. The silhouette was unique – two widely separated pairs of split uptakes. No fewer than 20 Kashins were built for the Soviet Navy and three more for India, the *Rajput*, *Rana* and *Ranjit*.

The Kashins have proved successful, and have appeared around the world. However one, the

F301
F 301

Otvazhny, was lost in the Black Sea in September 1974. She suffered some sort of internal explosion and caught fire, burning for five hours. According to various sources, including the Russians themselves, combustible materials such as plastics generated large quantities of smoke, and casualties are believed to have been nearly 300 dead.

Because the Soviet Navy has no aircraft carriers as such, the air defense role is not yet of prime importance, although of course individual major warships are equipped to defend themselves. Thus the Kynda and Kresta I type cruisers carry Goa missiles, while the Kresta II and Kara types carry the later Goblet missile. Since then the big nuclear cruiser *Kirov* has appeared with a new missile codenamed SA-N-6 by NATO. What makes it unusual is that it is vertically launched from 12 forward positions, although clearly more than 12 missiles are carried. The successor to the Kara class, the 8000-ton *Sovremennyy*, has been to sea without weapons, and although a new pattern of 130mm gun has since been added, along with anti-submarine SS-N-14 missiles, the new SAM has not been identified. Western intelligence sources credit the SA-N-6 missile with a ceiling of about 100,000ft, a slant range of 40 miles, a 200 pound warhead and a speed of Mach 6. This should be taken as the 'worst case', but it shows how missiles have been improved.

Left: The Sparrow air-to-air missile was adapted to provide US Navy ships with the Sea Sparrow short range air defense system.
Below left: The Norwegian destroyer escort *Bergen* fires a Penguin antiship missile from its quarterdeck canister.
Below: A number of the Soviet Kotlin class destroyers have been rebuilt as air defense ships and are now known to NATO as the SAM Kotlin class.

So far the air defense systems talked about have been long and medium range area defense systems. By their nature these missile systems are not good at coping with targets which fly low, and inevitably a defense has had to be found against aircraft and missiles which 'leak' through the outer layers of protection. This was formerly left to fast-firing guns, but the growing dominance of guided weapons in the 1960s and 1970s resulted in guns disappearing from NATO warships. As early as the 1950s the British had investigated the idea of adapting air-to-air missiles to defend ships, in a project called 'Hot Shot', but it was the Americans who persevered with it. The Sparrow missile was adapted to be launched from an 8-cell box mounted on top of a 3inch gun pedestal, and christened the Basic Point Defense System. 'Point defense' is the modern term for close range defense, as opposed to area defense. From this concept other developments followed, notably Improved Point Defense Missile System (IPDMS) and NATO Sea Sparrow, and today a number of navies use variants of these.

The Italians, who manufacture Sea Sparrow launchers for NATO, decided to redevelop the Sparrow, and within the same airframe provided improved electronics for a family of three missiles, all known as Aspide. With only minor changes Aspide is used as an air-to-air weapon, a ship-mounted point defense weapon and a land-based air defense weapon. In its naval version the Aspide missile is fired from an Albatros system, and it is compatible with the original NATO Sea Sparrow, requiring only minor modifications to convert from one type of missile to the other.

The British, after abandoning their 'Hot Shot' program, decided in 1951 to develop a simple missile defense for ships. The range was to be 5000 yards, outside the range to which aircraft had to close before launching their weapons, and for simplicity visual Command to Line of sight was chosen as the method of guidance. Under the codename 'Green Light' test vehicles flew in 1955, and a contract was signed in 1958. The system, known as Seacat, went to sea in the destroyer HMS *Decoy* in 1960, and in July 1962 became operational in the destroyer *Barrosa*.

Seacat was designed to cope with targets having a slow crossing rate, and although this remained adequate for some years the Royal Navy knew that the

Above: The twin Terrier missile launcher of the Italian cruiser *Andrea Doria*. In the background, one of the ship's AB.204B antisubmarine helicopters.
Above left: HMS *Norfolk* fires an Exocet during trials of the weapon system in 1974.

new generation of aircraft targets would require something better. Furthermore the Soviet Navy was known to be introducing new types of antiship missile. In 1964 a Naval Staff Target for the Seacat replacement was drawn up. Known as Confessor, the project was undertaken by Hawker Siddeley Dynamics and British Aircraft Corporation, and full development by BAC began in mid-1968. In 1969 six vertically launched test vehicles (quaintly codenamed 'Sinner') were fired from the old frigate *Loch Fada*, but the decision was made to use a more conventional 6-cell above-deck launcher. The new weapon, now known as Sea Wolf or GWS.25, went to sea in the frigate HMS *Penelope* in 1976, and the first operational warship to receive the new system was the frigate *Broadsword* in 1979. Sea Wolf used many ideas developed for the land-based Rapier system, principally the concept of a 'hittile', a small missile agile enough to guarantee a very high probability of hitting its target, rather than relying on a proximity burst. In fact Sea Wolf was given a proximity fuze to increase its effectiveness, but it retains the original Rapier qualities of ultra-fast acceleration off the launcher and a spectacular agility against rapidly maneuvering targets.

The performance of the missile would be needed, for in 1968, the year in which development began, the Soviet Gorky shipyard delivered the first Charlie class attack submarine. Western intelligence observers noted with interest the eight hatches in the forward casing, which concealed a new antiship cruise missile capable of being launched underwater. Here was an alarming new dimension to the surface threat, a missile which could be fired from well inside the normal range of air defenses. In theory a Charlie could slip inside a task force's screen, and the first the defenses would know would be when the SS-N-7 missile popped up out of the water and headed straight for the largest object detected by its radar seeker.

The electronics of Sea Wolf could be made

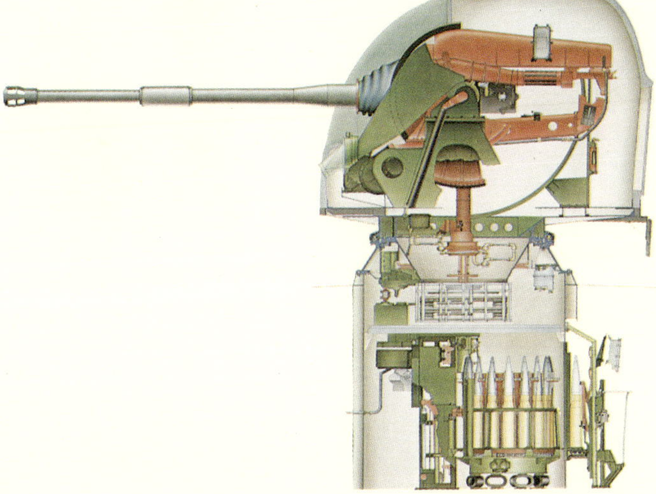

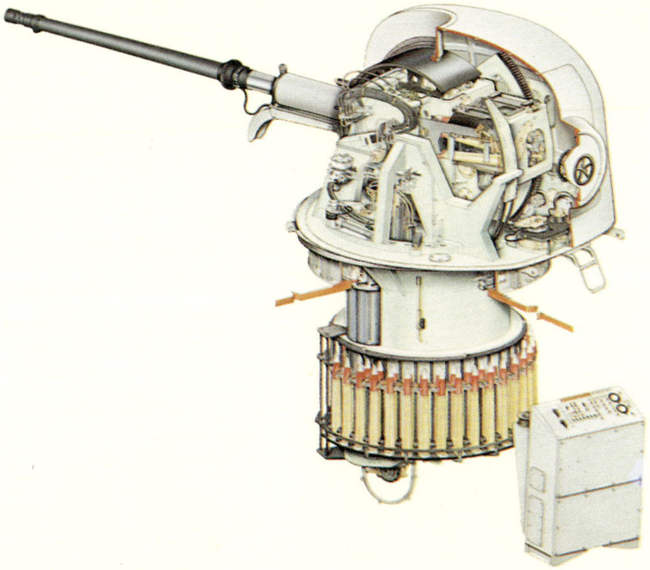

Above: The Vickers 4.5-inch Mark 8 gun is the Royal Navy's standard weapon for gunfire support.
Above right: The OTO-Melara 76mm compact gun is now in service with the US and several other navies.
Below: The US Navy has adopted the 20mm Phalanx Gatling gun as a Close In Weapons System for last ditch defense.
Left: The six-cell Sea Wolf launcher in B position aboard HMS *Broadsword* appears insignificant but its missiles can knock down an aircraft or missile out to 5000 yards.

capable of handling the data sufficiently fast to allow a rapid response to a 'pop-up' missile, but it would take no fewer than five computers. Two radars were provided, the D-Band pulse-doppler Type 967 capable of detecting targets up to 75 degrees, and the E-Band monopulse Type 968 capable of detecting low level targets. To speed up the data-rate the radars are mounted back-to-back, and rotate 30 times per minute. In theory the GWS.25 system is ready only 5–6 seconds after the 967/968 radars detect a target, and unless the operator countermands the order, a missile will be fired automatically. As it accelerates to Mach 2 it is 'gathered' into the beam of the Type 910 I/J-Band tracker, which is tracking both the missile and its target. Commands to the missile are sent through a microwave link, and two missiles can be handled by the tracker simultaneously. In cases of extreme sea clutter or jamming control can be handed over to a TV camera boresighted to the 910 tracker.

To provide the sort of reaction time needed the Sea Wolf system has been made automatic, but as a safety device the control system will only generate an automatic response to a target behaving like a missile flying toward the ship, ie a small diameter, high speed target on a collision course. This means that the system is programmed to ignore passing aircraft and helicopters.

Unlike other point defense systems, Sea Wolf has been tested in action, having been fired by both the *Broadsword* and her sister *Brilliant* in the fierce air-sea battles around the Falklands in 1982. One alarming discovery was made in the engagement which resulted in the sinking of HMS *Coventry*; the computer program had not allowed for two air targets weaving and crossing over, and a firing solution was delayed as a result. Fortunately modern computer software is

comparatively easy to alter, and discovery of such a shortcoming does not invalidate the whole system.

The drawback to the Mk 1 version of Sea Wolf is that the weight of the tracker and below-decks equipment restricts its use to large warships. The *Broadsword* class frigates displace over 4000 tons, and have a 'double-headed' system with two launchers and two trackers; the smaller *Leander* class and the new Type 23 could only take one launcher and tracker, as well as the masthead radars. A Mk 2 version has a lighter equipment, and the new Lightweight Sea Wolf will achieve a much greater reduction of weight.

The Russian point defense system is known to NATO as SA-N-4, and it differs in having a twin-arm launcher which pops up from inside a cylindrical weatherproof housing set in the deck. Photographs of the SA-N-4 out of its housing are rare, but it is believed that the missile reloads are stowed around the inside of the cylinder. It first appeared in the Kara class cruisers and the Nanuchka class missile corvettes, but has since been fitted in a wide variety of ships. Its successor may already be in service in the latest classes, in a vertically-launched configuration.

The attraction of vertical launch is that it dispenses with bulky loading systems and launchers, all of which are as complex as any gun mounting and therefore constitute an additional drain on manpower, both to operate and maintain. If a missile can be embarked as a 'wooden' round in a sealed container, and simply dropped into a hole in the deck it will always be ready to fire. There are, of course, drawbacks to vertical launching, which is why it has taken so long to be perfected. For one thing, it had to wait until the design of the missiles themselves and their electronics had progressed to a point where they could be left unattended in a sealed container for months on end. Another difficulty was the stress on the missile exerted when it swings through as much as 90 degrees from its launch-trajectory to its flight path. Modern thrust-vector control has overcome the problem, but it has proved necessary to provide extra boost to make up for the loss of range in 'gathering' the missile back into the guidance beam. The US Navy has now adopted vertical launch for the Standard missile, and the later *Ticonderoga* class cruisers and the *Arleigh Burke* class destroyers will dispense with the twin-arm Mk 26 launchers.

A vertical launch version of Sea Sparrow has also been developed, and was recently tried in the Canadian destroyer HMCS *Iroquois*. With point defense systems the virtues of vertical launch are even more obvious; the comparatively small missiles can be sited to cover all four quadrants. The next generation of warships will be designed to take more advantage of vertical launch, whereas the current ships were designed with conventional launchers in mind. The British have returned to the idea of a vertically-launched Sea Wolf, and designs have been prepared

Above: Soviet Kanin class destroyers are modifications of the Krupnyi class with SA-N-1 Goa missiles.
Above left: The US Navy's standard medium caliber gun for the 1980s is the 5-inch Mark 45.
Below: The Soviet fleet oiler *Desna* refuels a Kara class cruiser. The missiles abreast of the Kara's bridge are SS-N-14 stand-off antisubmarine weapons.

for a 40 round system. If it is ready it will go into the Type 23 frigates, and it can be retrofitted to the existing Type 22 (*Broadsword* class).

The French Navy has developed its own point defense missile, a 'navalized' version of the land-based Crotale. This uses an 8-cell launcher with its own on-board radar tracker. Crotale Navale is now operational in the *Georges Leygues* class 'corvettes' and is being retrofitted to older surface ships. Like the British Sea Wolf it is a bulky system, and the designers have drawn up plans for lightweight versions. Although not claimed as an antimissile system when introduced, the Mk 2 version has been upgraded to allow it to engage sea-skimming missiles.

The final form of point defense is the gun. Once regarded as virtually useless, it has made a remarkable comeback, and the reason is not hard to find. The cost of missiles is so high that even practice firing has to be restricted, whereas gun ammunition is comparatively cheap. What has also changed is the accuracy of fire control; guns can derive the same benefit from computers and modern electronics as any missile system. The gun has therefore returned to warships in recent years, not as a medium range weapon but as a 'close-in' defense against missiles and aircraft which have evaded the outer layers of defense. To put it bluntly, the morale of sailors demands something capable of shooting at close range targets, rather than mere reliance on chaff launchers and jamming.

179

D80

Above: A Soviet Kynda class missile cruiser 'riding herd' on the USS *John F. Kennedy* and her escorts.
Above left: The Soviet Kanin class DDGs are designed to provide air defense for task groups. Like their US equivalents they are 'double enders' with separate missile systems fore and aft.
Below: The British DDG HMS *Sheffield* on builder's trials in 1975. She was sunk by an Argentinian ASM early in the Falklands conflict.

There are several solutions to the problem. One school of thought favors a 'wall of lead' simply interposing sufficient metal to penetrate the warhead, guidance system or rocket motor of a missile to disable it. The other approach is to use larger projectiles with proximity fuzes to detonate close to the missile. Both methods rely on getting sufficient hits on the sensitive parts of the missile, 'splashing' it into the sea or detonating the sensitive warhead. The risk is always that large fragments of the missile will 'go ballistic' and continue on the same course to crash into the ship, but supporters of gun systems claim that the hail of metal will almost certainly destroy such large pieces of wreckage.

The best known close-in gun system is the Phalanx, a naval version of the 20mm Vulcan 'Gatling' or revolving aircraft cannon which first saw action in Vietnam. The Phalanx is an autonomous system which is bolted to the deck, and merely requires an external power source. A radar on the mounting tracks not only the incoming target but the stream of 20mm rounds (fired at a rate of 3000 per minute), and by 'closed loop spotting' fires the gun when the target reaches a predetermined spot some 3000 yards away. The Phalanx has shown its capabilities by shooting down a Walleye laser-guided bomb, and it is now being fitted in all US Navy surface combatants. During the Falklands fighting five Phalanx mountings were supplied in great haste to the Royal Navy, one for shore training and two each for the carriers *Invincible* and *Illustrious.* It is also used by the Japanese Maritime Self Defense Force and other navies. A new 4-barreled 30mm version is under development.

The Russians have also adopted a 'Gatling' type of point defense gun, a 30mm mounting which can be seen in most large combatants; it has replaced an earlier 23mm 'Gatling', presumably to give greater stopping power. The number varies from eight mounted in the *Kiev* and *Minsk*, down to one in the Grisha class light escorts. Unlike the Phalanx they have a separate fire control system, known to NATO as Drum Tilt.

Also in the 30mm range are such weapons as the Oerlikon twin 30mm, which is also made in Britain by their subsidiary B-MARC. As already mentioned, the heavy air attacks by Argentine aircraft led to the hurried installation of twin B-MARC 30mm guns as well as single 20mm. The only limiting factor was the restricted space available in the DDGs, which had to sacrifice their boats to make way for the guns amidships.

The Italian company Breda Meccanica Bresciana came up with a different solution. In conjunction with the Selenia and Elsag companies they produced the Dardo point defense system, using a twin 40mm Bofors gun mounting controlled by a low-level fire control system. The guns are in fact license-built versions of the original Swedish 40mm L/70 and they

Above: The *Sovremennyy* is the lead ship of a new Soviet class of 'large antisubmarine ship'.

Below: The West German *Bremen* class frigates (*Bremen* is shown) have the same hull as the Dutch *Kortenaer* class but different propulsion and electronics.

fire specially designed proximity-fuzed and pre-fragmented ammunition designed to riddle a missile with tungsten balls. What Breda has done is to provide a very advanced feed system, which allows the guns to fire 300 rounds a minute from each barrel. Such a rate of fire has to be seen to be believed, and firing trials against simulated sea-skimmer targets show a remarkably high rate of 'kills'.

For those customers who adhere to the 'wall of lead' philosophy Breda has produced a similar mounting with twin Mauser 30mm guns. The Dutch company Signaal has developed a system known as 'Goalkeeper', originally with four 30mm Mauser guns but later with a General Electric GAU-8A revolving 30mm gun. It resembles the Phalanx in having its own radar on the mounting. Goalkeeper is undergoing trials before delivery to the Royal Netherlands Navy, and is under consideration by the Royal Navy and the Federal German Navy.

The latest and in many ways the most advanced system is the multi-national Sea Guard. Oerlikon-Buhrle provided a quadruple 25mm mounting with an unusual skewed trunnion to permit shooting close to 90 degrees overhead, while Contraves provided the tracker, Siemens the processing and Plessey the C-Band missile-detecting radar. Testing of the individual components was complete in 1982, and the first fully engineered system is to start trials in 1984. As a genuine example of international cooperation Sea Guard could be a great success, and the Royal Navy is known to be looking at it as a successor to the Phalanx. An alternative is Sea Dragon using the GAU-8A 30mm 'Gatling', a Sea Wolf tracker, a Swedish C-Band radar and a Vickers gun mounting.

A totally different approach is offered by the Ram system, a joint American-German development for the defense of fast patrol boats. Using the Phalanx mounting General Dynamics provided a Rolling Airframe Missile (RAM), while various German companies developed subsystems. The advantage of the rolling airframe is that it provides accurate response to commands with only a single guidance channel. The missile homes passively on the radar seeker of an incoming missile, and when detection is achieved it switches to infrared homing. The appeal of Ram is that it can cope with multiple attacks, and because of its simplicity and the use of many off-the-shelf components its price is considerably cheaper than most point defense systems.

The great conflict between the sea-skimming missile and the various point defense systems remains nothing more than a war of words so far. Neither side is prepared to submit to a 'shoot-out', for a decisive result would be a public relations disaster for one or other. However the success of Exocet in the Falklands must push the leading navies into the expense of a full-scale trial sooner or later, to establish whether there is a credible defense.

6. ANTI-SUBMARINE OPERATIONS

The Sikorsky SH-60B SeaHawk is a new helicopter designed to operate from frigates, destroyers and cruisers of the US Navy. This SeaHawk is attempting to land, on the flight deck of a frigate which is maneuvering at high speed, with the aid of the RAST haul-down system.

The growing power of the submarine has inevitably led to a great increase in the amount of money spent on antisubmarine warfare. ASW, as it is known, has changed little in basic principles from the techniques by which the Allies defeated the German U-Boats in 1943–44; close escort for formations of merchant ships or warships, distant escort to bring support where it is needed, long range maritime patrol aircraft, and above all, integral air support for the close escort. What have changed beyond all recognition are the techniques.

In both World Wars there was a divergence of opinion about the basic strategy for fighting submarines. The 'offensive' school wished to pursue submarines wherever they might be, a strategy which is described today as wide area hunting. The second school of thought wanted to concentrate shipping so that warships could defend them when U-Boats attacked; what is called a covering strategy today. From 1914–17 the 'offensive' school held sway, and literally thousands of British and French ships of all sizes scoured the seas in vain for targets, while merchant ship losses climbed steadily, to the point where Britain was in danger of being forced out of the war.

In April 1917 the strategy changed to one of convoying shipping, and the change seemed truly miraculous. Losses fell while sinkings of U-Boats climbed rapidly. From near-defeat in April 1917 the Allies reached a point in October 1918 where the U-Boats were suffering 40 percent losses. The reasons were twofold: the U-Boats were forced to come to the convoys, where they faced well-armed escorts, but equally important was the fact that a U-Boat would only have one chance to fire torpedoes before taking evasive action. Previously U-Boats had cruised on the surface, using deck guns to sink small targets, and only submerging to avoid detection. Convoying forced the U-Boats to operate submerged for longer periods, robbing them of easy targets and limiting their endurance.

When World War II started the British had no reservations about convoy, but in the United States Navy the offensive strategy had many supporters. The six months after Pearl Harbor came as a rude awakening, therefore, when U-Boats inflicted enormous casualties on American shipping off the East coast. Once again convoy provided the solution, and thereafter the US Navy put its massive resources into developing ASW escort forces. The major difference from World War I was the important part played by aircraft. Shore-based patrol aircraft were fitted with a range of specially developed sensors such as short waveband radars and magnetic anomaly detectors to hunt U-Boats, while close support was provided by smaller aircraft operating from small utility aircraft carriers sailing with the convoys.

As the massive Allied building programs got into

Above: A US P-3 Orion maritime patrol aircraft drops the new Mark 50 lightweight torpedo during development trials.
Left: The Danish destroyer *Peder Skram* has been modernized with eight Harpoon missiles in B position and NATO Sea Sparrow SAMs aft.

full swing in 1942–43 it was possible to move to a more offensive strategy, using support groups of escorts (often with a small carrier providing local air support) to harass U-Boats before they reached the convoys, or to reinforce the escort of a convoy under attack.

There was another element in antisubmarine warfare. In World War I the British had been able to read radio messages to the U-Boats and to pinpoint positions by direction-finding, but until the advent of convoy the methods of counterattack were too crude to achieve worthwhile results. In World War II, however, a similar cryptographic 'break-in' yielded immense benefits, once sufficient hunting groups and maritime patrol aircraft were available. In effect these 'Ultra' intercepts enabled detections and kills to be made over a wider area than before, before the U-Boats got to grips with their victims. This advantage was aided by a British technical innovation, a high-frequency direction-finding set small enough to be put into a warship; escorts could trace the source of a radio transmission, even if they could not read the signals.

It was one thing to know of the whereabouts of a U-Boat, but quite another to sink it. In 1914–18 all ASW was hampered by the lack of an underwater sensor; a crude hydrophone helped to redress the balance, but nothing much would be achieved until the British perfected their Asdic, the precursor of modern sonars. Throughout World War II Allied escorts used their active sonars to detect and classify underwater targets, and it remains the prime method of detection, although in different forms.

The first effective ASW weapon was the depth charge, a canister of high explosive detonated at a preset depth by a hydrostatic valve. At first depth charges were dropped over the stern of an escort but in World War II 'throwers' were used to form patterns of charges around the target. The next innovation was to drop them from aircraft. In 1943 the first homing torpedoes appeared, using passive receivers to steer the torpedo toward the noise of a U-Boat's propellers. Shipboard depth charge throwers were improved to permit charges to be fired ahead of the ship; this allowed the target to be held in the sonar beam throughout the attack, whereas previously the last stage of the attack had been made 'blind'.

In the past 20 years modern technology has enabled ASW forces to develop a wide-area strategy. It is called the SOund SUrveillance System (SOSUS), and comprises a network of hydrophones or passive

F184

7
20
24

Left: Eight Type 21 frigates were built for the Royal Navy in the early 1970s of which two were sunk in the Falklands. A shortcoming in their design was the use of aluminum in the superstructure to keep weight down. HMS *Ardent* is shown. Below: Three of the US Navy's missile frigates, *Oliver Hazard Perry (FFG.7)*, *Antrim* (FFG.20) and *Jack Williams* (FFG.24).

receivers laid on the seabed. By positioning the SOSUS arrays near 'chokepoints' through which hostile submarines must pass to reach their hunting grounds it is possible to reduce the area in which hunting forces, whether aircraft, ships or friendly submarines must operate. Any noises detected by the hydrophones are transmitted by cable to a shore station, where computer processing calculates the position, course, speed and even type of submarine. Within seconds the information is radioed back to the ships and aircraft acting as 'pouncers' inside the SOSUS barrier.

A maritime patrol aircraft receiving such a signal would begin a hunt for the target, using sonobuoys to localize the submarine still further. Sonobuoys vary in type, but broadly they are miniature receivers (some are active) which are parachuted into the water over a wide area, in the hope that two or more will give a 'fix' on the submarine. Their information is signaled back to the aircraft, whose processing equipment translates the signals into a plotted position. There are other methods of detecting a submarine from the air; magnetic anomaly detectors (MAD) can identify the distortion in the earth's magnetic field made by the steel hull of a submarine, and the Autolycus 'sniffer' can detect the diesel fumes of a snorkeling submarine from their infrared content. All methods have their limitations, but used in conjunction with one another they provide a means of detecting submarines, and there is, of course, radar capable of detecting the periscopes and snorkel masts of submarines moving close to the surface.

Having detected its target the maritime patrol aircraft (known as an MPA for short) would normally drop a homing torpedo, retarded by parachute to make sure that it enters the water at the most favorable angle. The torpedo immediately enters a preset pattern, usually a descending spiral, until the passive sensor in its homing head detects propeller noise. It then tracks the target's noise and steers itself to impact. The previous generation of acoustic homing torpedoes, notably the American Mk 37, Mk 44 and Mk 46, have small warheads designed merely to blow off a submarine's propeller. Nowadays, however, it is reckoned that a missile-firing submarine might well launch its deadly strategic missiles as a last gesture of defiance before sinking. The latest 'lightweight' (air-dropped) torpedoes are therefore designed with a heavy warhead capable of sinking the submarine with a single shot. The British Stingray takes the process further by being programmed to hit the submarine amidships, and uses a special shaped charge to penetrate the titanium outer skin of the latest Russian submarines. Its American equivalent, the Mk 50 Advanced Light Weight Torpedo (ALWT) will presumably use similar techniques to enhance its killing power.

The majority of Western homing torpedoes are built with some degree of interoperability; the Mk 44, Mk 46, Stingray and Italian A.244 all have a diameter of 324mm (12.75 inches) to enable them to be fired from the standard Mk 32 triple launcher used aboard ships, as well as being dropped by aircraft. The particulars for the Mk 46 give some idea of the characteristics of today's homing torpedoes:

Diameter: 12.75 inches (324mm)
Length: 102 inches
Weight: 568lbs (dry)
Range: 12,000 meters at 45 knots
6000 meters at 40 knots

The higher speed is used for shallow running (50ft), but at 1500ft the speed and range decrease accordingly. The Mod 0 version used a seawater battery but Mod 1 (weighing 508lbs) uses Otto liquid fuel. The longer Mk 50 ALWT will weigh an estimated 800lbs, presumably because of its higher speed which demands more fuel.

Torpedoes are mainly used against submarines operating down to medium depth (down to 1500ft), but something more potent is needed against modern deep-diving submarines, which can exceed the 2000ft mark, and are even credited with a diving depth of 3000ft in some cases. The first weapon designed to function at maximum depth was the fearsome nuclear depth charge codenamed 'Betty', introduced in the 1950s. With an all-up weight of 1243lbs 'Betty' was too big to be lifted by most naval aircraft, and even the Grumman S-2F Tracker had its bomb bay enlarged to house it. The next generation was 'Lulu', otherwise known as the Mk 101 depth charge, which could be lifted by a helicopter. Advancing techniques of manufacture led to the Mk 105, christened 'Little Lulu', which is currently in service.

The workhorse among Western maritime patrol aircraft is the P-3 Orion, a four-engined derivative of the Electra turboprop airliner which entered service in 1958. It serves widely throughout the West, and has gone through many variants. The latest is the Canadian CP-140 Aurora, which uses the same airframe to accommodate more modern sensors and equipment. In addition to the US Navy, Orions are in service with Australia, Canada, Iran, New Zealand, Norway and Spain. Its predecessor, the twin-engined P-2 Neptune is still serving with Argentina, Brazil, Chile, Japan and Portugal, but in the Netherlands it has been replaced by the French Atlantic.

The Dassault-Breguet Atlantic was built to meet a NATO requirement for the Neptune successor, but only Germany backed the French in joint production as other nations insisted on their own design. However

The Japanese Maritime Self Defense Force has built a series of light escorts of the *Chikugo* class of which the *Iwase* (DE.219) is a unit.

the Dutch and the Italians finally came into the program, and a New Generation Atlantic is coming forward, capable of carrying more payload and having more modern detection equipment.

In going their own way the British ended up with a very expensive but efficient maritime patrol aircraft. The MR.1 Nimrod was adapted from the Comet IV airliner, and is unique among shore-based aircraft of this type in having turbofan engines – four Rolls-Royce Speys. Like other ASW aircraft the Nimrod has been modernized to take advantage of new technology, and the airframe has been adapted as an Airborne Early Warning radar platform. The 50ft bomb bay of an ASW Nimrod can carry a wide range of stores, including Mk 46 or Stingray torpedoes, mines, 'Lulu' nuclear depth charges, conventional bombs and fuel tanks. Two or four underwing pylons also carry air-to-surface missiles such as Martel. In the Falklands conflict in 1982 several Nimrods operating from Ascension were hurriedly armed with the air-launched version of the American Harpoon antiship missile. They achieved no successes, largely for lack of targets, but it shows the versatility of large maritime patrol aircraft.

The US Navy uses twin-engined antisubmarine aircraft from its big carriers (CVs). For many years the standard ASW airframe has been the Grumman S-2 Tracker, a remarkable aircraft capable of providing radar search as well as strike functions in one. Its replacement is the S-3 Viking, which like the Nimrod, uses turbofan jet engines to provide power for rapid transits, but without excessive fuel consumption. So comprehensive is its outfit of sensors and processing equipment that their total cost is more than double that of the airframe.

The Russian equivalent of the P-3 Orion is the Ilyushin Il-38, known to NATO as the May, but it compares poorly with its Western counterpart, and has not been developed further. This is largely because of a differing Soviet philosophy, which concentrates more resources on reconnaissance aircraft, to provide data for coastal units. Being a huge landmass, the Soviet Union has no need to sustain its war economy with imports, and so will not need to protect shipping in the way that NATO must. However, with a growing tendency by the Soviet Navy to practise the techniques of projecting power overseas, sea communications will become more important, and it seems likely that the Soviet Navy will have to switch some of its resources from surveillance to active ASW.

The 'pouncer' ships operating behind the SOSUS barriers are equipped with antisubmarine helicopters. The concept dates from World War II, when attempts were made to spot U-Boats with helicopters operating from freighters, but exploitation of the helicopter had to wait until the machines themselves had advanced in design. The British developed the MATCH system in the 1950s, using a light helicopter from a flight deck on the stern of a 2000-ton frigate to deliver torpedoes. The Canadians, however, were more ambitious and put a bigger HSS-1 helicopter onto a frigate, allowing the use of a 'dunking' sonar to search for submarine contacts well away from the ship. The US Navy tried to compromise between these extremes, using a remote-control drone called DASH to deliver torpedoes to the point of sonar contact.

DASH was a good idea, as it avoided the risk of losing valuable pilots, but it was probably too advanced for the technology of the day. Some two-thirds of the drones were lost accidentally, and they came to be regarded as highly suspect by ASW specialists. Perhaps the faults could have been eradicated, but so much money had been spent that the system was finally withdrawn at the end of the 1960s. The fiasco had unfortunate consequences for the US Navy, for it had to wait another decade before light helicopters were again accepted as vital components of an ASW escort's equipment, whereas in the meanwhile other navies had built on the British and Canadian success.

The *Esmeraldas*, seen here running trials without her antiship missiles, is one of a class of six built in Italy for the Ecuadorian Navy.

Above: A Krivak I class frigate shadowing the carrier USS *Coral Sea* in the Indian Ocean.
Right: The Saudi missile corvette *As Siddiq*, one of nine built on Lake Erie. She is armed with Harpoon missiles, a 20mm Phalanx CIWS and a 76mm gun.

The debate today is not whether or not a helicopter is necessary, but whether to have one or two. Helicopter facilities in a frigate-sized ship place a great burden on the design, for a hangar must be provided to protect the delicate machine from weather damage. The light alloys used in the aircraft are subject to corrosion, and so the helicopter must be washed down with fresh water before it goes into the hangar. The deck must be clearly lit for night-time operations, and there must be adequate fire-fighting facilities, as well as safety measures for refueling. A big helicopter such as the Sea King or the SeaHawk needs a 'haul-down' device to tether the helicopter during its final landing movement, and to restrain it once it is on the deck. Lighter helicopters like the Dauphin and Lynx require only a restraining device, a harpoon deck-lock which engages a mesh grille in the deck.

The first helicopter designed for operating from small flight decks was the remarkable Westland Wasp. Weighing only 3232lbs empty (5500lbs fully loaded) it is not a great weightlifter, but it can carry two Mk 44 homing torpedoes or rockets, machine guns or wire-guided antitank missiles. This allows the Wasp to be used either as a weapon-delivery vehicle in conjunction with the ship's sonar, or as a support aircraft for troops ashore. The best example of the ground support role was in the Falklands, when the British recaptured the island of South Georgia from Argentine forces. Two Wasps from the Antarctic patrol ship HMS *Endurance* used their antitank missiles to disable the submarine *Santa Fe* off Grytviken. The AS-12 missiles are guided by an optical sight.

The Wasp was intended for small frigates, but for larger ships the Wessex (derived from the American S-58) could lift more payload. The 150 HAS.3 ASW versions built were given a radar capable of tracking submarine snorkel masts; others were configured to lift assault troops or simply as air-sea rescue machines. Its successor is the Sea King, which used the US Navy's S-61 airframe as a basis for development. After experience with the Wasp and Wessex the Royal Navy reached the conclusion that the antisubmarine helicopter should become more independent of the operating ship if she was to develop her full potential.

The HAS.1 version of the Sea King incorporated not only the weapons (four homing torpedoes or an equivalent weight of depth charges) but also a 'dunking' sonar, doppler navigation radar (to permit accurate navigation away from the carrier or the shore), a search radar, autopilot and automatic hovering system. In addition the helicopter has a small tactical center in which the sonar and radar operators can exchange information and plot target data. On the antisubmarine screen a pair of Sea Kings is reckoned to be the equivalent of a frigate, for they can switch position quickly to meet a fresh threat. The latest version of the Sea King, the Mk 5 can drop sonobuoys, and carries an electronic data processor to sift the information coming in from sonobuoys. The maximum range of a Sea King is in the region of 937 miles (1507km) when loaded, and the maximum ceiling is 10,000ft.

Both the Wasp and the Sea King are due for replacement, the Wasp having become operational as long ago as 1962 and the Sea King seven years after that. The Wasp replacement, the Anglo-French Lynx, has already proved itself to be an outstanding machine, but the Anglo-German-Italian Sea King replacement, designated EH.101 is still under development. The Westland/Aerospatiale Lynx is equipped with a Seaspray radar which enables it to use Sea Skua antiship missiles as an alternative weapon-fit to depth charges or torpedoes. During the Falklands fighting two Lynxes fired the then untested Sea Skua (preproduction rounds had been hurried into service) against three Argentine ships. It is officially claimed that a salvo of four missiles sank a large patrol boat, while a salvo of two crippled another patrol craft and a single hit disabled a third craft. In its antisubmarine role it can carry a 'dunking' sonar (the French Navy uses its Lynxes in this way) or act as a delivery-system, in much the same way as the Wasp.

The US Navy, having been let down by DASH, was understandably nervous about asking for funds for another ASW helicopter, and the first LAMPS (Light Airborne Multi-Purpose System) did not appear until 1970. The helicopter, the SH-2 Seasprite, is regarded one of the world's best-designed and neatest solutions to the problem, and the SH-2D carries more than two tons of equipment, including a powerful 'chin-mounted' radar, sonobuoys, MAD gear, electronic warfare receivers and jammers, and a variety of weapons, including depth charges and torpedoes.

Fortunately the escorts which had operated the DASH system retained their small hangar and flight deck, and it proved possible to enlarge the hangar to accommodate the Seasprite. The frigates of the *Knox* class, for example, all operate a Seasprite, and others are deployed aboard cruisers and destroyers. In all the US Navy operates six Light ASW Helo Squadrons for the ship-flights, and keeps two Readiness Squadrons for training. The original SH-2D version is now superseded by the SH-2F, with improved sensors and rotors to enhance all-round performance.

A proposal to build a LAMPS II came to nothing, and the US Navy has gone straight onto LAMPS III, the Sikorsky SH-60B SeaHawk. This big machine is closer to the British idea of an airborne autonomous

Right: A French escort firing her Dagaie decoy launcher to create clouds of metallic chaff and flares to decoy radar guided or heat-seeking antiship missiles.
Below: The SA-N-3 Goblet antiaircraft missile launchers on the fo'c'sle of the Soviet helicopter carrier *Moskva*.

857

Above: The Soviet fleet oiler *Boris Chilikin* refueling the helicopter carrier *Moskva* (right).
Right: The new Soviet destroyer *Udaloy* strongly resembles the US *Spruance* type not only in layout but also in design philosophy, with some weapons sacrificed to improve seakeeping and habitability.

ASW platform, rather than a mere weapon-carrier, for it carries a comprehensive outfit of sensors and weapons. Unlike the British and other European navies, however, the American ASW philosophy maintains that the processing of sonar, MAD, sonobuoy and radar returns is better carried out aboard the parent ship. The SeaHawk accordingly transmits its data back to the ship, and receives instructions about prosecuting contacts, rather than operating independently.

Although the Soviet Navy has an impressive record in helicopter developments the current generation of Russian naval helicopters does not bear comparison with Western counterparts. The Kamov Ka-25 Hormone-A in payload or performance lags behind the Seasprite, for example, and has been in service since 1965. A replacement, the Ka-27 Helix, was first seen in Exercise Zapad '81 held in September 1981, aboard the new *Bolshoy Protivolodochny Korabl* (large antisubmarine ship) *Udaloy*. Like the American *Spruance* class, to which she bears a strong resemblance, the *Udaloy* has a double hangar aft. There is little of startling novelty in the Helix but its more capacious fuselage undoubtedly accommodates more weaponry and sensors than before.

The operation of antisubmarine helicopters in Western navies is to a large extent standardized. In a specialized ASW carrier like HMS *Invincible* there will be 14 duty Sea King crews, each containing two pilots, an observer and an aircrewman. A sortie may take up to four hours. During that time the Sea King may be maintaining a sonar 'watch' to screen the carrier and her escorts from attack, or she may try her team's skills against a target submarine playing the part of 'clockwork mouse'. Although the Sea King, like all helicopters, demands a lot of maintenance, well-trained maintainers can keep them flying. During the Falklands Campaign the pilots of 820 Squadron, embarked in the *Invincible* broke all previous records; by the end of June 1982 they had flown 5000 hours, 300 percent more than their normal flying hours. This phenomenal effort included not only ASW screening for the Task Force but also air-sea rescue missions, vertical replenishment of stores from ship to ship, and the unpleasant task of acting as decoys against the threat of missile-attack.

Although all US Navy escorts are capable of detecting and attacking submarines, the primary ASW platforms are the frigates of the *Knox* and *Oliver Hazard Perry* classes and thc *Spruance* class destroyers. The 46 *Knox* (FF.1052) class were built in 1965–74, the largest single group of surface combatants since the Russian Skory class destroyers in the 1960s. They are attractive ships, with a big single 'mack' amidships; the main armament is an 8-cell Asroc missile-launcher, from which Harpoon antiship missiles can also be fired. Mk 32 torpedo-launchers in the superstructure provide a quick reaction against submarines, and the SH-2D/F helicopter is an extension of the ASW systems, exploiting the long range of the bow-mounted SQS-26CX sonar. The ship also carries a single 5inch gun and a Sea Sparrow system.

The *Perry* (FFG.7) class were intended to meet criticism that the *Knox* class lacked armament, and were accordingly given a mix of ASW and AAW systems. They carry a single-arm Standard SAM launcher forward (like the Asroc launcher it can also launch Harpoon SSMs). Instead of Asroc they carry two SeaHawk helicopters (the later ships), and in addition to the SQS-56 sonar in the bow they have the new TACTASS (TACtical Towed Array Sonar System). This new type of sonar, which can be operated by submarines as well as surface ships, provides the first big advance in submarine detection since the advent of medium range active sonars after World War II. In simple terms it is a line of low-frequency hydrophones mounted in a flexible tube towed at a considerable distance behind the ship. This distance enables the array to be kept clear of the noise of the towing ship's propellers.

A towed array can be up to several hundred meters long, and it provides a series of detection 'funnels' or 'beams' capable of detecting the low-frequency noise made by submarines. The biggest advantage of towed arrays is the phenomenal distance at which submarines can be detected, but they impose new operational and tactical restrictions on ASW ships. In the 1970s a typical escort force might have been composed of maritime patrol aircraft in close support at about 30 miles' range, helicopters operating their 'dunking' sonars at about 15 miles, and frigates forming a close screen at about five miles. Today the same aircraft, using the new directional sonobuoys and processors as capable as those in the surface ships, are more likely to be 100 miles out or more. The towed array ships will take up a new mid-field distance of about 50 miles, leaving a small number of escorts to handle the close range screen against any submarines which sneak through the outer and middle layers of protection.

This new style of ASW can be extended by using submarines' towed arrays out to as much as 200 miles' range, but this opens the area of operations to something in the region of 125,000 square miles. Assuming that sufficient forces are available to exploit these tremendous detection ranges, there is bound to be great difficulty in coordinating the efforts of ASW forces working in three dimensions. Many previously-held ASW doctrines must be questioned. Are ships in a typical 15-knot convoy (as against the 11-knot average in World War II) better protected by towed array escorts in direct defense or by stationing them widely apart to protect a 'sanitized zone' or defended lane? It is also open to question whether current escorts can handle a flow of information from such a wide area; 'non-submarine' contacts must be classified just as thoroughly as genuine contacts, if only to avoid waste of effort in prosecuting a search. There is also the question of whether to invest in tactical towed arrays like TACTASS, which offer easily processed detection, or to go for longer range surveillance (called SURTASS), performed by small, slow ships.

The pioneers in towed arrays are the US Navy and the Royal Navy, which shared development. Nuclear hunter-killer submarines are already using the BQR-15 and BQQ-5 (US Navy) and Type 2023 and Type 2024 (RN), and the British Type 2024 is reported to have given excellent results in the Falklands. The French, Dutch and Japanese Navies are all introducing towed arrays, and it is only a matter of time before other navies follow suit. The Royal Navy's *Broadsword* class frigates are fitted with Type 2031, and this set is also being fitted to some *Leander* class and the new Type 23 *Daring* class frigates.

When announced the *Spruance* class destroyers provoked bitter criticism for their apparent lack of armament. On a length of 563ft and a displacement of 7800 tons full load, the critics could not understand why the ship carried only two single 5inch Mk 45 guns, an Asroc missile-launcher and two triple torpedo tubes. What they ignored was the careful attention paid to quietness, efficiency as a helicopter platform, and above all, room for the installation of future equipment without the need for drastic reconstruction. Since completion the ships have received Sea Sparrow short range missiles aft and Harpoon antiship missiles, and there are plans to fit them with Tomahawk cruise missiles and Phalanx close-in weapons.

The most advanced feature of the *Spruance* design is their gas turbine propulsion, with four General Electric LM-2500 gas turbines driving two shafts. Great attention is paid to quiet running, with special mountings to reduce radiated noise, a Prairie-Masker device to reduce cavitation noise from the propellers, and sound-absorbent material around the bow sonar dome. The big beamy hull is very seaworthy, allowing sonar contacts to be pursued in rough weather and facilitating helicopter operations. When they first went to sea from 1975 onwards the ships operated a single SH-3 Sea King, then two SH-2 Seasprites, but in due course they will receive two SeaHawks.

The British *Broadsword* class frigates are designed to much the same philosophy. Although smaller than the *Spruances* their 4500-ton hulls emphasise seakeeping and steadiness as helicopter-platforms. As with the American ships they encountered bitter criticism from within and outside the Service, and as recently as mid-1981 it was openly advocated that the

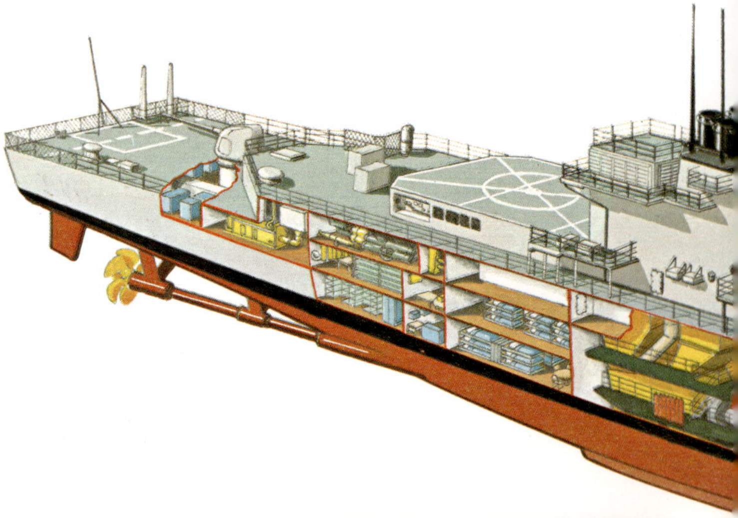

Below: Cutaway drawing showing the armament and internal design of the *Spruance* class destroyers. Note the bow sonar dome.

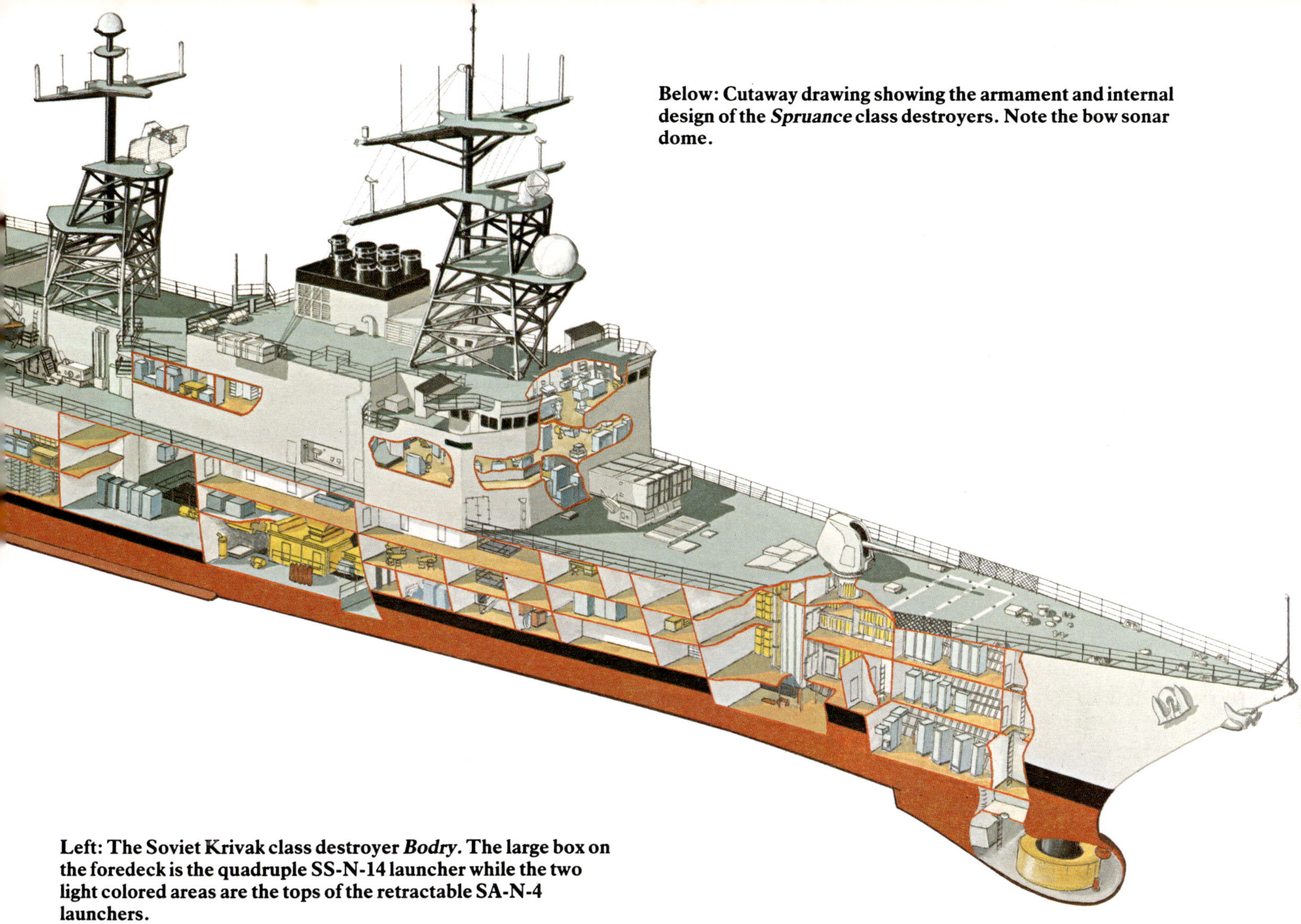

Left: The Soviet Krivak class destroyer *Bodry*. The large box on the foredeck is the quadruple SS-N-14 launcher while the two light colored areas are the tops of the retractable SA-N-4 launchers.

Left and below: Two of the *Spruance* class destroyers. Left, the *Spruance* herself and below the *Caron*. By early 1984 there were 31 *Spruance* class ships (DD.963-92 and DD.997) in service with the US Navy.

class should be cut short at seven units. Two years later, after experience in the Falklands seven more were on order. They are intended to work with the three *Invincible* class ASW carriers in mid-Atlantic, acting as 'pouncers' behind the SOSUS barriers in the GIUK Gap. For that purpose they are equipped with the Type 2031 towed array sonar, a hull-mounted Type 2016 low-frequency passive sonar and two Lynx helicopters armed with Stingray torpedoes. To defend themselves against surface-, air- or submarine-launched missiles the first eight ships have MM-38 Exocet antiship missiles, and a double-headed Sea Wolf short-range missile system.

In the Falklands the *Broadsword* and *Brilliant* had little opportunity to show their skill as submarine-hunters but they coped magnificently with the appalling weather conditions and their Sea Wolf systems proved lethal. TV film exists of *Brilliant*'s Sea Wolf tracker locked onto an Argentine Mirage III over San Carlos Water, and both ships scored 'kills'.

The Royal Navy hoped to retrofit Type 2031 and Type 2016 sonars to ten of the *Leander* class frigates, but as explained previously, the essence of towed array operations is the elimination of ship noise, and after the first four conversions it was realized that silencing their steam turbines was far too expensive. The decision was then made to cut back the conversion program, and to build instead a new class of frigate, the Type 23, suitably silenced at the design stage. To achieve the degree of silencing required the designers chose three Rolls-Royce Spey gas turbines for main drive, with a separate diesel-electric unit for quiet running while operating the towed array.

The Dutch *Kortenaer* and *Van Speijk* class frigates will also operate towed arrays, but will use the American SQR-18 set. The French, who have for a long time used a combination of bow sonar and variable-depth sonar from the stern, hope to have their own towed array, the ETBF at sea in the fifth and sixth *Georges Leygues* class destroyers, which are planned to go to sea in 1985–86. These 4000-ton ships are very similar in general configuration to the British *Broadsword* class, being armed with four MM-38 Exocet missiles, two Lynx helicopters and a point-defense missile system. Previous French ASW ships were armed with the Malafon stand-off missile, but the *Georges Leygues* class rely on the Lynx helicopters to deliver torpedoes. Instead of an all-gas turbine propulsion system they have Rolls-Royce Olympus gas turbines for full speed and diesels for cruising.

The standard US Navy ASW weapon is the RUR-5 Asroc, which uses a solid-fuel rocket motor to lift it into a ballistic trajectory out to six miles. The payload is either a Mk 17 nuclear depth charge or, more usually a Mk 46 torpedo which is released to parachute into the water shortly before impact. Its submarine counterpart is Subroc, which is fired from a torpedo tube in a canister, fires itself from the canister when it broaches the surface and follows a ballistic path some 30–40 miles to the target. There it functions like Asroc, releasing a nuclear depth charge (a torpedo-carrying variant never materialized). Today Subroc is obsolescent, and is being phased out in favor of the Mk 48 heavyweight torpedo, but a replacement, the Stand-Off Weapon (SOW) is under development. This will have alternative torpedo and depth charge payloads from the outset, but it is too early to give any precise information about how the weapon will work.

Mention has been made of homing torpedoes, and for many years the US Navy's Mk 44 and Mk 46 weapons have been standard among Western navies. Two countries, Britain and Italy, have developed new homing systems compatible with the dimensions of the American torpedoes, the Stingray and the A.244, which means that they can still use the standard triple Mk 32 launching tubes. Other countries like Sweden and France continue to develop their own torpedoes.

Older British warships mount the Mk 10 Limbo mortar, a three-barreled weapon capable of firing a pattern of depth charges about a mile. Limbo, like other weapons of the same vintage, went out of favor as it was massively outranged by sonar, but in the Falklands the need for a 'scare' weapon was felt. The basic British tactics were to use submarines for distant screening with towed arrays, and for escorts to use active sonar as a deterrent to the two Argentine diesel-electric submarines. The theory was that if the hostile submarines detected active 'pinging' and if all contacts were depth charged the assumption would be that a hunt was on, and the submarine would break away to avoid attack. Whether this stratagem was successful is not known, but the British reported only one submarine attack on the Task Force, and only one ship was hit by a 'dud' torpedo. The only weapon which can be used to 'scare' attacks in this way is the depth charge, for a homing torpedo which does not acquire a target sinks harmlessly to the bottom, and exercises no deterrent effect whatsoever.

The British also use a stand-off weapon to make use of increased sonar ranges. The Ikara was developed jointly with the Australians, and is basically a small pilotless delta-wing aircraft, carrying beneath it a Mk 44 or Mk 46 torpedo. Like Asroc it suffers from having too little range to work effectively with modern sonars, and plans to boost its range were not pursued. However it remains a potent weapon, and is mounted forward in the DLG HMS *Bristol* and many of the *Leander* class frigates. The three Australian DDGs *Perth*, *Brisbane* and *Hobart* have two Ikara

Above right: An SH-2F Seasprite landing on the flight deck of the USS *William V. Pratt* (DDG.44).
Right: The new Soviet naval helicopter, the Helix, on the flight deck of the *Udaloy*.

HV
50
NAVY
HSL-32
9032
50
50
H

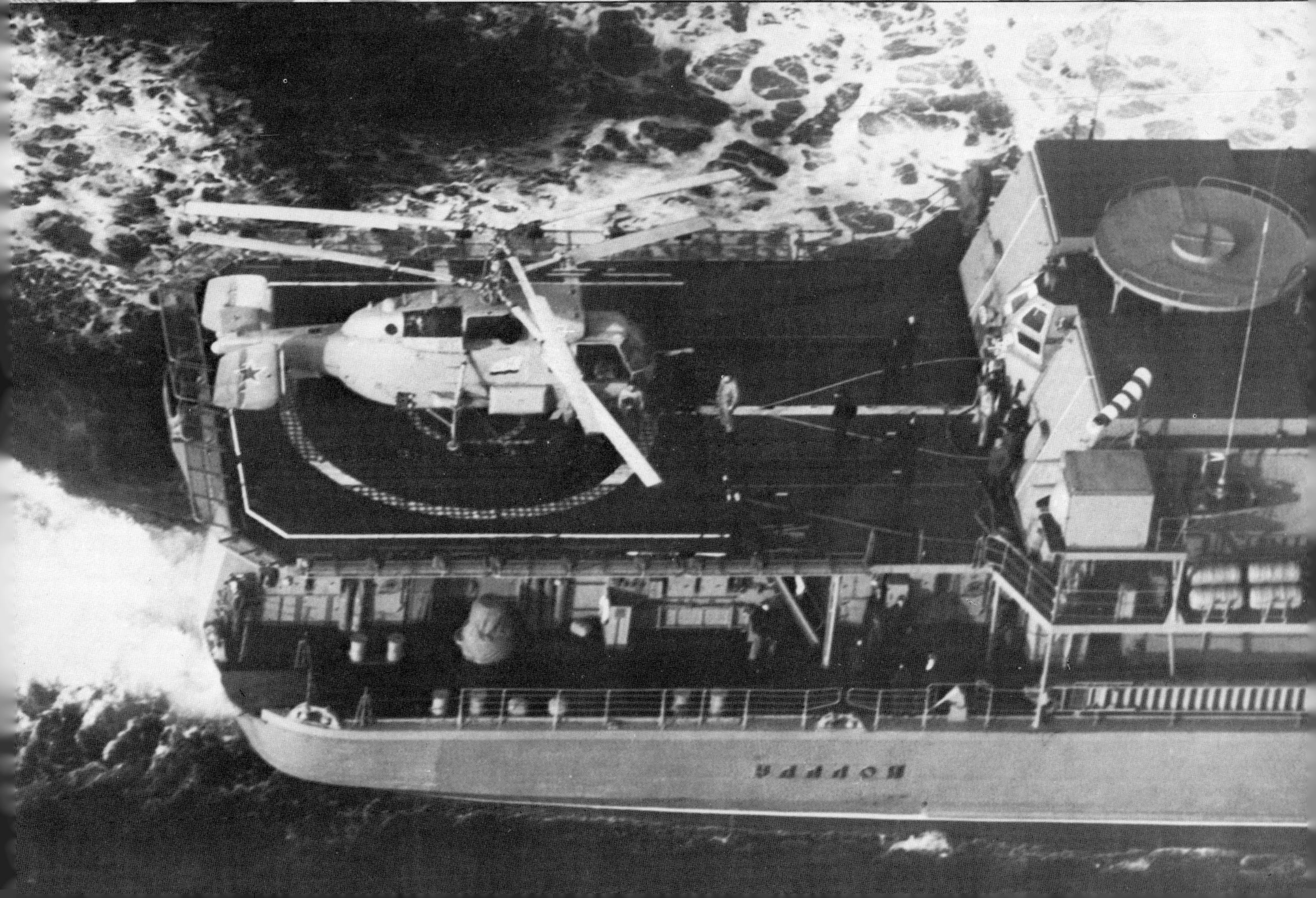

TG
DANGER
ROYAL NAVY
43

Above: A French Navy Lynx dropping a Mark 46 acoustic homing torpedo. The braking parachute has just started to open and the retaining straps are falling clear.
Left: A Westland Sea King helicopter winching up its Type 195 dipping sonar.

launchers amidships, and their 'River' class destroyer escorts mount a single launcher on the starboard side aft. Unlike Asroc, Ikara is under positive command from the moment it leaves the ship, and can be 'flown' to a fresh interception point if the target shifts position rapidly. Once over the target area the delta-wing carrier breaks into three sections, allowing the torpedo to parachute into the water.

The French equivalent, named Malafon, uses a rocket to launch the missile, which then glides to the point of detection before releasing its homing torpedo.

Many navies still use the Bofors 375mm rocket-propelled depth charge, either from twin launchers or from multiple launchers. The French built their own six-barreled launcher to fire these rockets, and the Norwegians developed the Terne system for their destroyer escorts. The old standard depth charge rolled off the stern has now virtually disappeared from warships, if only because sonars are now sufficiently precise to make such crude methods unnecessary.

It is interesting at this point to contrast the Soviet approach to ASW. For some years Western observers concentrated on the Soviet Navy's anticarrier forces, failing to notice a significant shift toward antisubmarine warfare. With hindsight the reason is not hard to understand; as the threat of nuclear attack from carrier-borne bombers receded the threat from SSBNs was becoming more credible. By 1964, with ten Polaris SSBNs at sea and a new class of 31 boats under construction, the Soviets had reason to think that the Americans had transferred their nuclear strike effort from carriers to SSBNs. It can hardly be a coincidence that in 1963 two antisubmarine cruisers (*Protivolodochny Kreyser*) were laid down. The ships, named *Leningrad* and *Moskva* are clearly intended to take a large number of ASW helicopters to sea, as their half-length flight deck and hangar allow a total of 15 to 18 Kamov Ka-25 Hormone-As. In this they were only following the precedent set by the French with the *Jeanne d'Arc* and the Italian *Andrea Doria* class and the *Vittorio Veneto*.

The forward part of the hull is devoted to armament, being separated from the flight deck by a massive centerline superstructure. A heavy defensive armament of 44 SA-N-3 Goblet SAMs is mounted, with two twin-arm launchers, backed up by two twin 57mm gun mountings, one on either side of the superstructure. The antisubmarine armament includes a hull-mounted low-frequency sonar and a medium-frequency variable-depth set streamed from a well under the quarterdeck. For close range defense against submarines two pairs of 12-barreled rocket launchers are mounted forward. Originally two sets of quintuple torpedo tubes were mounted low down in the hull amidships but these were removed in the late 1970s, probably because they were flooded out in heavy weather. These tubes were almost certainly for antiship torpedoes, rather than homing types, as the main offensive ASW weapon is the FRAS-1 (Free Rocket Anti Submarine, or SUW-N-1 in its NATO designation) rocket launcher. It resembles Asroc in being a ballistic rocket, but is launched from a twin-arm launcher, with an estimated 20 rounds in a magazine below. It is credited with a range of 16 miles, and Western sources claim a nuclear warhead for it, and no alternative payload.

The next step in the evolution of Soviet ASW was the adaptation of the Kresta cruiser design to the antisubmarine mission. The *Kronshtadt*, first of a new class designated Kresta II in the West, differed in having a new long range antisubmarine missile in place of antiship weapons. Muddled perception of Soviet intentions led Western intelligence sources to spend seven years trying to identify a new long range cruise missile known as SS-N-10, but finally the quadruple launch tubes on either side of the Kresta II's superstructure were admitted to be holding an

Three maritime patrol/antisubmarine aircraft. Above, the French Atlantic Nouvelle Generation, left, the British Nimrod MR.2 and, below, a Soviet Il-38 May shadowed by an F-14. Each aircraft carries MAD equipment in a tail boom.

Ikara equivalent designated SS-N-14. Although the reported range of 25 miles may be on the high side, it may be intended to receive inflight corrections from helicopters and maritime patrol aircraft.

Although also rated as a large antisubmarine ship, the Krivak class which followed a year after the first Kresta II was a smaller and simpler ASW escort. The Soviets are not alone in wanting to find cheaper alternatives to first rate ships, but unlike the major Western navies they deliberately aim for a 'hi-lo' mix, using second rate or utility ships to eke out the small numbers of first rate ships. Confusion over the SS-N-10/SS-N-14 missiles caused the Krivak to be greatly overrated in the West, but finally Western sources agree that it is an austere ASW escort armed with four SS-N-14 missiles and driven by two gas

Main picture: The Nigerian frigate *Aradu* was built by Blohm and Voss on the MEKO principle, using containerized weapons and sensors to permit rapid exchange of faulty equipment or modernization.
Above right: A torpedo-armed SH-60B SeaHawk showing the dispenser for sonobuoys above the torpedo mounting.
Far right, top: An SH-3A Sea King helicopter lowering its dipping sonar. This type of sonar search is aided by the fact that the helicopter generates no underwater noise.

F 89

turbines at a speed of 30–31 knots. Apart from two sets of quadruple torpedo tubes put in for traditional reasons rather than to meet any serious tactical requirement, the remaining armament is defensive: two twin 76mm AA guns, and two SA-N-4 point defense missile systems. The Krivak II, which appeared in 1976, substitutes single 100mm guns for the twin 76mm, and updated fire control, but otherwise differs little. Twenty of the Krivak Is were built in three shipyards, followed by 11 Krivak IIs, and production appears to be continuing.

The 'demotion' of the Krivaks from BPKs (large antisubmarine ships) to *Storozhevoi Korabl* or SKRs (large patrol ships) was taken by some observers to indicate that the Soviet Navy had somehow been disappointed in the design. This does not appear to be the case, for it is almost certainly Russian views on antisubmarine warfare which are changing, and we can expect designations of ships to change as well. The Russians appear to have given up ideas that they had previously of taking the offensive against Western SSBNs in distant oceans. Instead they are looking at ways of securing a safe passage for their own SSNs and SSKs through Western ASW barriers such as the GIUK Gap, and of safeguarding their SSBNs in 'bastions' close to their main bases. The support of antibarrier operations would call for a ship with much stronger defensive armament than the Krivak, but that type of escort would be well suited to defend the

Above: The Soviet Kresta II class cruiser *Marshal Voroshilov* has SS-N-14 antisubmarine missiles as her main armament but also two twin SA-N-3 antiaircraft missile launchers, a Hormone-A helicopter and a range of guns, torpedo tubes and rocket launchers to enable her to operate in distant waters. All 10 Kresta IIs were built in the Zhdanov Shipyard in Leningrad.
Below: The guided missile frigate *Oliver Hazard Perry* (FFG.7) commissioned in 1977. She is the lead ship of a large class of 3500-ton escorts which carry a mixed gun and missile armament and two antisubmarine helicopters.

'bastions', particularly if working with shore-based aircraft.

The next class of large warships was the Kara class, an expansion of the Kresta II, but driven by gas turbines instead of steam. There is visible evidence of an improved outfit of sensors, notably a variable-depth sonar, like the one in the *Leningrad* and *Moskva*, and the Krivaks, and the seven Karas seen so far represent a great improvement in appearance, at least when compared with the two Kresta classes. Like the Kresta II they have eight SS-N-14 missiles in two quadruple banks disposed on both sides of the bridge.

The appearance in 1976 of what appeared to be an aircraft carrier caused consternation among Western navies, and many observers believed that the Soviets had at long last built an attack carrier. But the *Kiev* and her sisters *Minsk* and *Novorossiisk* turn out on close examination to be yet another permutation in the Russian battle to master Western SSBNs.

The *Kiev* design is a hybrid cruiser/support carrier, equipped primarily to operate Ka-25 Hormone-A antisubmarine helicopters, but with a flight of Yak-36 Forger vertical takeoff strike aircraft to provide local air superiority and to force hostile surface forces to keep their distance. An interceptor/strike aircraft would permit a Soviet ASW group to operate in hostile waters, beyond the range of land-based fighters. The most likely area of operations is the North Atlantic, where any Soviet surface group trying to clear NATO forces from, say, the GIUK Gap and its SOSUS barriers, would come under attack from US carrier battle groups and shore-based strikes. Although equipped with the trademarks of a conventional carrier, a starboard 'island' superstructure and an angled flight deck, the *Kiev* class devote the entire forward section to what might be termed 'cruiser qualities', eight tubes containing SS-N-12 antiship missiles, a FRAS-1 (SUW-N-1) missile launcher, a twin 76mm gun mounting, two RBU-6000 multiple rocket launchers, one of two SA-N-3 Goblet systems and an SA-N-4 point defense system, to say nothing of the associated fire control directors and radars. As in the helicopter carriers, the *Kiev* was completed with two sets of 533mm (21inch) torpedo tubes low down and well forward, but this questionable feature was not present in her sister *Minsk*, so presumably it had proved susceptible to weather damage and was suppressed.

The latest major antisubmarine unit in the Soviet inventory is the new destroyer named *Udaloy*. First seen in 1981, the *Udaloy* is radically different from previous Soviet designs. In fact she bears a strong resemblance to the US Navy's *Spruance* class, in having a big hull with comparatively few weapons (by Soviet standards), and enhancing the antisubmarine warfare at the expense of other roles. It is ironic that the Soviet designers appear to have grasped the necessity to build seaworthiness into ships rather than merely packing weapons into a hull, just as a rising tide of largely ill-informed criticism in the West demands more weaponry 'like the Russians'.

The standard Russian antisubmarine weapon is, as we have seen, the SS-N-14 missile, which equips all the major ASW ships. For close range defense there is the RBU-6000, the latest in a series of multiple rocket launchers, but smaller patrol craft are also armed with a lightweight 400mm torpedo similar to Western homing torpedoes. The FRAS-1 missile has already been mentioned; Western observers regard it as a weapon suitable only for a 'hot' all-out war, using the massive destructive power of its nuclear warhead to sink submarines, even if the comparatively inefficient Soviet sonars have not been able to pinpoint the target. The same argument can be applied to Subroc in US submarines, of course, and it is equally difficult to imagine an occasion short of World War III on which an American escort would fire a nuclear-tipped Asroc missile.

One feature of Soviet ASW which is not matched in the West is the way in which small coastal escorts are used to surround a target before simultaneously bombarding it with rockets. Film of Soviet naval maneuvers shows this tactic clearly, and it conforms to other areas; whenever possible the Soviet aim is to position forces before mounting a coordinated saturation attack. It also implies an unwillingness to concede any tactical initiative to the man on the spot.

7. MINES AND MINESWEEPERS

The Federal German Navy's inshore minesweeper *Hertha* enters the British port of Harwich. The sweep gear aft is painted yellow to aid recovery.

As naval warfare becomes embroiled in an upward spiral of mounting costs it is hardly surprising that navies have turned back to one of the oldest and most cost effective weapons – the mine. What is surprising, on the other hand, is that until recently only the Russians appeared to show any great interest in mine warfare.

Mines were used as long ago as 1776, when David Bushnell's primitive keg mines were used on the Delaware River to deter the redcoats. It went down in history as the 'Battle of the Kegs' and 80 years later the Russians laid chemically-fuzed mines in the Baltic. They were cast-iron conical mines, and a small field laid in the approaches to Kronstadt damaged the British sloop *Merlin* in 1855. Only six years later in the Civil War the hard-pressed Confederacy tried to match Northern naval strength with a series of ingenious mines, known at the time as 'moored torpedoes'. Admiral Farragut may have said 'Damn the Torpedoes', but these primitive devices sank the monitor *Tecumseh*.

Mine warfare came of age in the 20th Century, when both the Japanese and the Russians used them with deadly effect in 1904. The two World Wars saw an enormous increase in not only numbers but efficiency of mines. The statistics were staggering; in World War II the British alone laid nearly 80,000 offensive mines which sank or damaged 1917 Axis ships. Overall one mine in 40 was effective, but in some areas efficiency rose to one in five; mines laid by aircraft proved seven times as effective as bombing, torpedoes or any other form of air attack. In Germany 60 percent of seagoing naval personnel were employed on minesweeping, close escort or harbor duty. The

British started the war with 70 minesweepers, and by increasing this to more than 1500 by 1944 succeeded in holding losses down to 500 merchantmen and 281 warships.

The most frightening aspect of mine warfare today is that the successes of World War II were achieved by relatively simple mines, whereas today's mines are many times more deadly and harder to sweep. Then the moored mine could be swept by cutting its mooring wire and letting it float to the surface. Trawlers could be commandeered from the fishing fleet and converted quickly. Then came the magnetic mine, first used by the British in the last months of 1918, but used in large numbers from 1939 onwards. Then, shortly after, came the acoustic mine, set off by the noise of a ship's propeller. Both types of 'influence' mine could be dealt with, one by sending a strong electromagnetic pulse through a towed cable, the other by towing a noise maker. This was not the case, however, with the 'oyster' or pressure actuated mine, which responds to the pressure wave set up as a ship passes through the water. No completely suitable way of simulating this pressure wave has ever been found, but fortunately, like the other influence mines, its use was restricted to shallow waters. Today most influence mines combine all three types of influence fuze, making the task of mine countermeasures yet more complex.

The British minesweeper support ship *Abdiel* is intended to support a squadron of mine countermeasures craft but she can also lay mines for exercise purposes.

In spite of the problems posed by German ingenuity in design of mines and antisweeping devices, the Allies finished World War II with a convincing margin of superiority over the mine; hundreds of wooden minesweepers had been built, the residual magnetism of steel ships' hulls could be reduced by 'degaussing', and apart from pressure mines in very shallow waters, the threat was under control. The first shock came in the Korean War, when the Russians supplied North Korea with magnetic influence mines of such sensitivity that even the World War II wooden-hulled sweepers could set them off – the actuator was sensitive enough to pick up the magnetism of the diesel engine and metal fastenings in the hull, for example. The big amphibious landing at Wonsan was held up for days by 3000 of these mines, and a startled US Navy reluctantly woke up to the fact that the Russians had lost none of their cunning in mine warfare.

The result was a panic program to build non-magnetic minesweepers in the early 1950s. On both sides of the Atlantic a new generation of wooden minesweepers was built, using non-magnetic metals such as phosphor bronze for anchors and other fittings. The ships of that program proved a great success and many are still in service 30 years later.

The biggest advance of the 1950s was the development of new techniques to cope with pressure mines and other influence types. The minehunter is a ship fitted with a high-definition sonar capable of detecting mines on the seabed in relatively shallow waters (60 meters or less), where influence mines are most effective. She steams slowly until she detects an object on the seabed, and then sends down a diver to investigate the contact. It may, of course, turn out not to be a mine, but a biscuit tin or similar piece of debris, but if it is a mine the diver lays a charge to be detonated alongside it, once he is clear of the scene.

Clearly the use of clearance divers involves an element of risk, and the diver is increasingly being replaced by a remotely piloted vehicle. This is similar to a tiny submarine, fitted with powerful lighting, a TV camera and a jettisonable demolition charge; it is

Above: The PAP.104 remote controlled mine disposal system is used by the French, British, Dutch and German navies.
Right: A US Navy MH-53E Super Stallion helicopter towing a minesweeping sled.
Far right, bottom: The French *Eridan* is the lead ship of the tripartite French, Dutch and Belgian mine hunter program.

maneuvered from the ship alongside the suspicious object, allowing the TV camera to photograph all around, and giving the specialists time to make an assessment. If the contact is finally classified as a mine, the remotely piloted vehicle is instructed to drop its explosive charge before returning to the ship.

The French Navy was the first to introduce such a vehicle, known as the Poisson Auto-Propulsé, the PAP-104, and it is now in service in the Royal Navy, the Royal Netherlands Navy, the Federal German Navy and several others. The Italians have developed the Min, which works on similar lines, the German Pinguin is a competitor, and the US Navy is developing its own, and within a few years the mine clearance diver will be a thing of the past.

The problem about such equipment is that it can no longer be fitted easily into the older minesweepers, for they also have to accommodate new electrical sweeps, towed noise generators and other bulky items. Instead it must be accommodated in specially designed and expensive hulls constructed out of non-magnetic material. However, minehunting remains a lengthy and maddeningly tedious business. The hunter must be prepared to spend at least 20 minutes on each sonar contact, whether it be a mine or a biscuit tin. As any skin diver knows, the seabed is littered with such objects.

There is an alternative to minehunting, the use of helicopters. The US Navy for many years put its faith in the large helicopter towing a 'sled' containing a noise maker or a turbine-powered magnetic sweep. This method was used to sweep the Suez Canal, and to clear the approaches to Haiphong at the end of the Vietnam War, but it has two big disadvantages. The helicopter is very vulnerable to the blast of a mine detonating underneath it; the machine is flying close to stalling speed, and the plume of water can strike the rotor blades, flipping the helicopter over, and in wartime there are not likely to be sufficient big helicopters available for large-scale sweeping. It is of course supremely flexible, in that helicopters and their equipment can be moved rapidly from one place to another, but it has so far provided no answer to the pressure mine. For that minehunting remains the only solution. Helicopters can also be used to hunt for mines, and the French have developed a suitable high-definition 'dunking' sonar, but the problem remains that helicopters are so valuable for other tasks that none may be spared in wartime for mine countermeasures.

The one remaining method not discussed is the

M641

hovercraft. Experiments show that the hovercraft is virtually immune to mine detonations, as the blast is vented outwards from under the rubber skirt. It has virtually no pressure, magnetic or acoustic signature, and so can cross minefields with little risk. Trials in Britain show that a big hovercraft can carry all the sweep gear, dipping sonar and plotting equipment needed for minehunting, and also sweep along a fixed line without any trouble. It is widely recognized that a minehunting hovercraft or MCH is not only feasible, but desirable as well, and all that prevents it from becoming reality is a shortage of money. However several hovercraft have been used to support mine countermeasures ships, and it is the next step.

The only inexpensive way of coping with widespread mining by a potential enemy is still the construction of minehunters, but 'inexpensive' is a relative term. The need to eliminate magnetism almost totally has meant a switch to glass-reinforced plastic (GRP), non-magnetic machinery, and even plastic knives and forks, a process which makes GRP minehunters the most expensive warships in the world, ton-for-ton. The numbers which can be built are therefore small; Britain is completing 12 *Brecon* class GRP ships, and is following them with a cheaper but less effective design. France, Holland and Belgium are building 25 'Tripartite' minehunters between them, and Italy is building 10 *Lerici* class. The US Navy is caught in a similar dilemma, having allowed its mine countermeasures forces to dwindle to 23 wooden ocean sweepers. Current plans allow for 14 *Avenger* class MCMs for long-distance work and 12 MSHs for coastal minehunting. They will be wooden-hulled with GRP superstructures (the MCMs) and GRP-hulled (the MSHs).

The British, always acutely aware of their vulnerability to mining of their harbors and estuaries, took the lead in developing the new type of craft. HMS *Brecon*, launched in 1978, displaces 725 tons, making her and her sisters the world's largest GRP warships. They are known as Mine CounterMeasures Vessels (MCMVs) to underline the fact that they undertake both conventional sweeping and minehunting. The propulsion plant includes two Deltic non-magnetic diesels for main drive at a maximum speed of 17 knots, and two hydraulic units for maneuvering at a maximum speed of 8 knots. The 60-meter hull is deliberately capacious, not only to accommodate the full range of equipment, but to provide adequate crew comfort on long voyages; an ability to make an ocean voyage was a prime feature of the Staff Requirement.

The size of the *Brecon* class led to considerable criticism until the Falklands, when the *Brecon* and *Ledbury* proved capable of making the 8000-mile voyage to the South Atlantic to sweep mines in Port Stanley. It was known that the Argentine Navy had a large inventory of modern mines, and two minefields were in fact laid in the harbor. In spite of adverse

Above: A Soviet Natya class minesweeper.
Left: Royal Navy divers during the clearing of the Suez Canal in 1974. In fact no mines were found.
Above right: The US Navy's wooden ocean minesweeper *Inflict*.

weather conditions and poor sonar conditions the two MCMVs had no difficulty in sweeping the mines. What came as a great surprise was that the only mines laid were Argentina-made copies of a German World War II moored contact mine – as always, the threat of mines is just as potent as their presence.

The Royal Navy intends to order 12 of the *Brecon* class, but their high unit cost and complexity of manufacture makes it necessary to build a 37-meter GRP 'single role' minehunter, without the extra size and lacking the ability to sweep for mines. They are to be known as the Gem class, and at least 12 are planned.

A word of explanation about sweeping is needed. Although the modern mine is always laid on the seabed, there is, as we have seen, a large number of conventional mines still in existence, and these may well be actuated by magnetic or acoustic influence. There is also the problem of the Continental Shelf Mine and the deep-laid antisubmarine mine. The Captor mine already exists, an encapsulated homing torpedo which is fired when a hostile submarine's propeller noise is detected. It can be laid by maritime patrol aircraft, and its chief role is to protect barriers such as SOSUS by denying choke points to hostile submarines.

The Intelligent Hunter Mine is an extension of the Captor concept, a torpedo (note how the words 'torpedo' and 'mine' are becoming interchangeable, as they were a century earlier) which can track a target some thousands of yards away. To dispose of such mines it is necessary to use a wire sweep, kept down to low-level by special apparatus. The mine is laid too deep for any actuator to be set off by magnetic or acoustic influence, so a steel hull may be used instead. At the end of 1978 the Royal Navy took over two commercial trawlers, the *Suffolk Monarch* and *Suffolk Harvester*, and converted them to Extra Deep Armed Team Sweep ships (EDATS). Under their new names, *St David* and *Venturer* they have been successfully operated by Royal Naval Reserve crews, providing a fresh source of trained manpower. A further 12 EDATS trawler-type sweepers, the River class, have been ordered, and they are intended to replace the ageing wooden coastal minesweepers and minehunters operated by the Royal Navy Reserve.

The French, Belgians and Dutch face the same mine threat as the British, but they chose to build their own design. The resulting tripartite program apportioned the work between all three countries, guaranteeing commonality of spares but at the same time ensuring that each country's industries are supported. The French naval design bureau, Direction Technique Constructions Naval had responsibility for overall design and French industry provided the minehunting sonar; the Dutch build the diesel engines and the Belgians manufacture the electrical equipment.

The lead ship, the *Eridan*, was built in an ex-German U-Boat pen at Lorient on the coast of Brittany. She joined the Fleet in 1982, followed shortly afterwards by the first Dutch ship, the *Alkmaar*, but difficulties with the consortium chosen to build the Belgian ships prevented the first order being placed until 1982. GRP construction requires a mold, and ships are normally built in pairs at intervals of up to a year. When the program is complete in 1988–89 a number of the older wooden minesweepers will be well beyond the age limit, and many will have been scrapped.

The Italians, like their European allies, favor GRP construction, and produced their own design. The ten *Lerici* class are 49.98 meters in length and displace 500 tons, making them slightly bigger than the tripartite design. They also differ from the British and tripartite ships in using a minehunting sonar of American origin, the SQQ-14, nicknamed the 'Squeaky Fourteen'. It is lowered on a chain through an aperture in the keel, whereas the British Type 193M and 2093, and the French DUBM-20A and DUBM-21A are hull-mounted.

The Federal German Navy has hitherto used a British sonar, the Plessey Type 193M in wooden coastal minesweepers built in the 1950s, but has now adopted a radically different 'Troika' system. This uses unmanned vessels under control from a parent ship, in order to avoid injury and loss of life. The principal component of the 'Troika', so called because three unmanned hulls are used, is a pressure-resistant conventional steel hull, whose diesel engine, controls, and power supply are on shockproof mountings. The magnetic clearance field is generated by two coils, which are positioned at each end of the hull. Acoustic mines are exploded at a safe distance by a pair of medium frequency noise makers in the bow section and an additional towed noise maker.

The control system uses a navigation radar to plot the positions of the three unmanned craft. The area to be swept is divided into sections, using radar-reflecting buoys as reference points. Coastal minesweepers of the *Lindau* class have been converted to act as Troika control craft, and six sets of 'drones' have been built, named *Seehund 1-3*. The prototype 'drones', christened *Seekuh 1-3* have already shown their resistance to underwater shock and blast in a series of trials held in the 1970s.

The FGN intends to follow the Troika mine countermeasures craft (although not capable of minehunting, they do carry wire sweeps) with ten Type 343 combined minelayer/minehunters to replace the existing *Castor* and *Schutze* class minehunters, which were commissioned in the early 1960s. What is even more intriguing is a plan for a Type 355 sweeper capable of sweeping pressure mines. If successful, these will be the first sweepers capable of dealing with the 'unsweepable' pressure mine.

On the opposite side of the world, the Japanese Maritime Self Defence Force is often overlooked as a powerful navy. The Japanese have not forgotten how the American mine offensive in 1943–44 virtually cut them off from raw materials and food imports. The *Hatsushima* and *Takami* class minehunters are equipped with a license-built variant of the British Type 193M minehunting sonar, designated ZQS-2, but differ from the latest European craft in being wooden hulled. The *Hatsushima* class, which have been coming into service since 1979, are equipped with Type 54 remotely piloted vehicles, similar to the PAP-104.

As already mentioned, the US Navy has only recently started the construction of minehunters, and

HMS *Brecon* lead ship of a class of mine countermeasures vessels. These are the largest glass fiber warships in the world and can sweep as well as hunt mines.

the keel of the *Avenger* (MCM.1) was not laid until June 1983. She and her planned 13 sisters will be 64.9 meters long and will displace 1032 tons, making them the largest mine countermeasures craft for 30 years. They will have an SQQ-30 dipping sonar, which is an improved version of the SQQ-14, and a new Mine Neutralization Vehicle (MNV) is under development. Like other minehunters the *Avenger* class and their small counterparts will be propelled by specially redesigned non-magnetic diesels, but the MCMs have a wooden hull; only the superstructure is made of GRP. One of the reasons for European shipbuilders switching to GRP as the alternative to wood for non-magnetic hulls is, sadly, that timber of the right quality from South-East Asia is likely to contain pieces of steel shrapnel. Wooden construction also brings in its train a substantial problem of maintenance, as even the most water-resistant timber will eventually succumb to rot.

The Soviet Navy's history of pre-eminence in offensive mine warfare has already been noted, but equally there is comparatively recent experience to remind the Russians about the need for adequate counter-measures. In 1949 the ex-Italian cruiser *Kerch* sank after being mined off Odessa, and six years later the ex-Italian battleship *Novorossiisk* sank with heavy loss of life in Sevastopol. It is reported that the state of mine countermeasures was so low that for some time there was no clue as to the nationality or age of the mines – the final verdict was that they were German magnetic mines left unswept after World War II, but the scandal was enough to ensure the dismissal of Admiral Kuznetsov, the Commander-in-Chief.

From 1947 to 1957 the Soviets built well over 200 seagoing minesweepers or *Morskoy Tral'shchik* of the T.43 type, 58-meter steel hulled 570-tonners. Most have been transferred to satellite navies, but others have been converted to radar pickets, tenders or handed over to the KGB Border Guard. They were succeeded by some 50 Yurka class, slightly smaller and built with an aluminum alloy hull. The Natya class (all names are code names assigned by NATO, not Soviet class names) are similar, but large enough to serve as coastal antisubmarine escorts as well. Since 1970 some 35 have been built, and they will presumably continue in production for some time. Compared to their Western counterparts they are heavily armed, with two twin 30mm guns, two twin 25mm heavy machine guns and two RBU-1200 quintuple antisubmarine rocket launchers.

From 1961–1973 seventy Vanya class coastal minesweepers, wooden hulled 39.9-meter craft rated as *Basovyy Tral'shchik* or base minesweepers, were built. Between 1967 and 1972 the two Zhenya class GRP sweeper/hunters appeared, but Western intelligence sources suspect that they were not a success as the larger wooden hulled Sonya went into quantity production instead. The first of these, named *Komsomolets Kirgiziy*, came into service in 1973, and at least 30 more have been built since then. In parallel a number of inshore minesweepers have been built, *Reydovy Tral'shchik* or roadstead sweepers, whereas the equivalent in Western navies, the inshore minesweepers built in the 1950s, were found to be too small to accommodate the necessary influence sweep gear.

The subject of minelaying has been left to last, for there is less variety in the methods used. In fact minelaying can be relatively unsophisticated, as mines can be laid from almost any platform. During World War II converted train ferries were used to lay defensive minefields, and destroyers and motor torpedo boats frequently laid mines off enemy coasts under cover of darkness. Before World War II special submarine minelayers had been built, but during the war mines were redesigned for laying through the standard 21inch torpedo tube. But the aircraft proved by far the best minelayer, able to sow large numbers of mines over a large area, and today it can be assumed that any widespread use of offensive minelaying would be done by aircraft. Submarines can lay minefields with less chance of detection but each submarine could only lay a maximum of 20 or so mines during a single mission, so a dense field would take months to build up.

The benefits of offensive minelaying demonstrate the effectiveness of this mode of warfare. When in 1972 US aircraft mined the approaches to Haiphong to prevent Warsaw Pact military supplies from reaching North Vietnam over a quarter of the Russian and Polish merchant ships sailed immediately. The mines were apparently activated on a time-delay, for none of the ships was sunk, but 26 ships which did not get out in time remained bottled up for a year. What is even more noteworthy is that the North Vietnamese Navy apparently lacked the knowledge to sweep the mines,

The *Enoshima*, one of the Japanese Maritime Self Defense Force's current *Hatsushima* class coastal minesweepers.

and had to leave the task to the Americans. It is no coincidence that the US Navy has since shown such interest in mine countermeasures, for it is widely believed that the Americans themselves had great difficulty in neutralizing their latest marks of mine.

In a more obscure instance a year later, Libya arranged for a minefield to be laid off her coast by the Egyptian Navy. Despite being partly in international waters its limits were not declared in advance, as required under International Law. Subsequently two merchant ships, one Greek and the other Lebanese, were sunk and a second Greek ship was damaged. The international reaction was surprisingly muted, but as always the ownership of the mines and the proof that Libya had instigated the minefield would have been very difficult to prove.

The threat from mines is so potent that the mere threat of mining can be sufficient to close a waterway. In 1974 the Suez Canal was reported to be blocked by mines and sunken ships, following the Yom Kippur War the previous year. In response to international demands to reopen the Canal Egypt permitted an international force, including American, British and Russian units, to undertake clearance. After a long and costly operation it was confirmed that the only explosive ordnance found was a miscellany of unexploded mortar bombs and other munitions dumped in the Canal by Israeli and Egyptian soldiers. Yet, to all intents and purposes, the Suez Canal had been closed to shipping, as if real mines had been laid.

Great secrecy surrounds the types of mines in service today, each side wishing to keep quiet about how much it knows about the other's mines. At least ten types of mine are listed in the inventory of the US Navy, and the development of new types is being pursued. The Mk 52 is a ground mine weighing 568kg, and capable of being laid by B-52D and B-52H bombers as well as Navy aircraft of various types. The various models have combinations of influence actuators. The Mk 55 is similar, but weighs 989kg and carries a heavier weight of HBX explosive. Both these are restricted to less than 50 meters' depth of water, whereas the Mk 56 has a more sensitive actuator, allowing it to be laid down to 350 meters. The Mk 57 is a 1012kg submarine-laid mine carrying 935lbs of HBX-3 explosive, and can be laid in 250 meters of water.

The Mk 60 Captor mine, already mentioned, has been under development since 1961 and is known to have encountered teething troubles in the early days. It uses a Mk 46 Mod 4 torpedo, and weighs 908kg. It is 3.66 meters long and is moored, in order to be laid at varying depths, being primarily an antisubmarine weapon. Its maximum depth is reported to be over 600 meters. The Mk 67 Submarine-Launched Mobile Mine is another advanced type of mine under development. It is apparently a converted Mk 37 Mod 0 torpedo which is fired from a submarine. Its purpose is to allow the submarine to lie off an enemy harbor at a safe distance, and to project mines into the harbor. It weighs 754kg and clearly any combination of actuators can be programmed to respond to the sort of targets which are to be attacked.

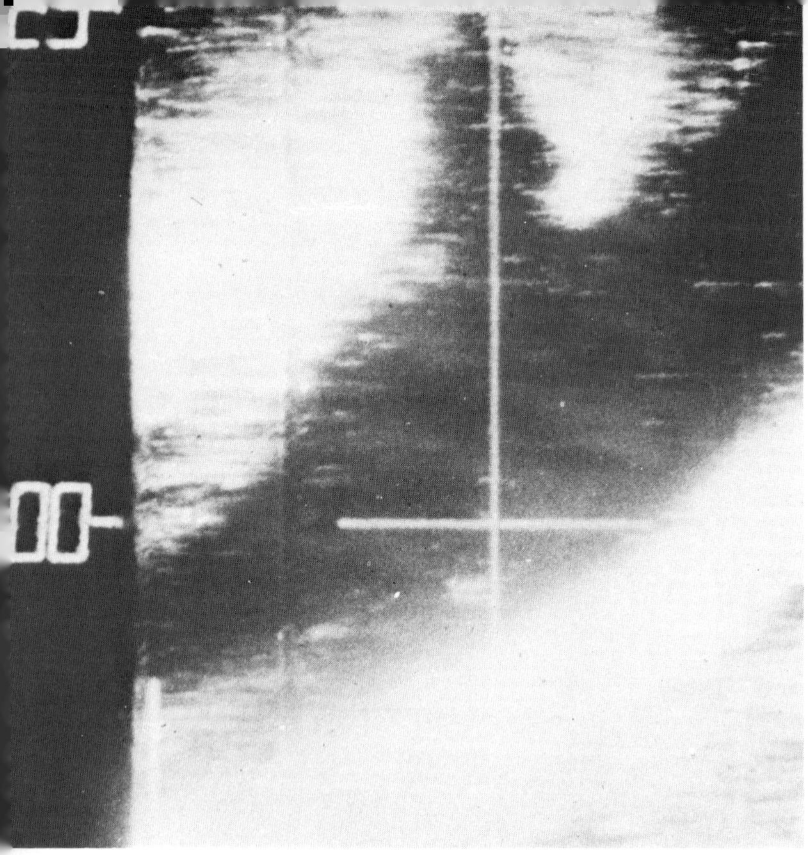

Above: What the minehunting sonar operator sees on his display – the shadow of a possible mine contact on the sea bed.
Right: NATO's STANAVFORCHAN (Standing Naval Force Channel) minesweepers operating in company with Dutch, Belgian, German and British ships present.

Some years ago work was in hand on a device known as the Propelled Rocket Ascent Mine (PRAM); the explosive charge was to be propelled upwards once the mine was actuated, bringing it into range of the target. Since then it has been succeeded by the Intermediate Water Depth Mine (IWDM), a moored mine capable of being laid out to the edge of the Continental Shelf to sink both surface ships and submarines. No further details have been released, but so much effort is being devoted in Western navies to countering the Continental Shelf Mine that we can only assume that it has realized at least some of its potential.

To replenish its long-neglected armory of mines the US Navy initiated the Quickstrike program, adapting the large numbers of 'iron' bombs left over after the Vietnam War. Three models of Quickstrike mine are known to exist: DST-36, converted from 500lb Mk 82 bombs, DST-40 converted from 1000lb Mk 83 bombs, and DST-41, converted from 2000lb Mk 84 bombs. All are fitted with magnetic actuators, while the DST-41 may also have a seismic actuator.

No US Navy surface warships are now fitted to lay mines, as the task is entrusted entirely to submarines and aircraft. In addition to 80 US Air Force B-52 bombers earmarked for minelaying the Navy's P-3 Orion, S-3 Viking, A-6 Intruder and A-7 Corsair aircraft are all capable of laying mines.

If the British public announcements are to be believed they possess no mines whatsoever, but it is known that several varieties of ground mine are in the inventory, and several more are under development including the Stonefish and the Sea Urchin. Both France and Italy are also active in the development of mines, and various models are exported to other countries. One of the mysteries of the Falklands Campaign was why Argentina made no use of the sophisticated British, French and Italian mines known to be in her possession. The only rational explanation is that they were being held in reserve in case of hostilities against Chile.

A totally new idea is being put forward, the Intelligent Hunter Mine, which consists basically of a mechanism to permit a mine to bury itself on being laid. This makes the mine very difficult to hunt or sweep, and less liable to drift. Like other modern mines, it can be laid in a deactivated state, and therefore need not be declared under International Law. Laying can be carried out over a lengthy period, when forces are available. As the mine has buried itself it will be very hard to detect, even if the potential enemy

suspects that a field has been laid. Not even the Deep Armed Team Sweep will make much impression on mines buried in silt or mud, and any remotely piloted destructor vehicle will have difficulty in 'seeing' them.

There are, of course, technical problems with such an advanced mine. The remote activation must be reliable and secure. It will be no use using a system which alerts the enemy to the fact that a detectable number of mines is receiving actuation signals. The actuation system must have some sort of fail-safe mechanism included in the circuitry, or else faulty mines could sink ships during peacetime or during a period of tension, and thereby precipitate war. There is no guarantee that these complex problems have been solved, but when they are, the intelligent hunter mine will become a reality.

Mines, whether moored or bottom-laid, can be laid by any surface warship with sufficient clear deck-space. The Baltic NATO navies, the Danish and Federal German, provide their destroyers, escorts and strike craft with mine rails to allow rapid conversion to the minelaying role. Normally a gun is removed to compensate for the additional weight, and the mines are simply hoisted aboard, the length of time depending on the size of ship and the number of mines to be embarked. Small ground mines can be rolled over the side, but the bigger types and moored mines (which include a heavy sinker) must be winched aft along the rails, and so the winch gear has to be installed as well. It is noticeable that all varieties of Soviet warship, from 15,000-ton cruisers down to minesweepers, are fitted with mine rails, an indication of the priority given to minelaying.

The capacity of the Soviet Union to wage offensive mine warfare remains a matter of conjecture, but it is unlikely that such a cheap and deadly method of harassing Western forces is being neglected. Western intelligence sources claim that 100,000 mines are kept in reserve, but clearly a large percentage of these stocks must be earmarked for defense. Even so, allowing for 75 percent allocated to the defense of harbors and key coastal points, 25,000 mines could be available for use against Western ports – a third of the total laid by the Royal Navy in five years of war, and eight times the number needed to stop a massive American landing at Wonsan in 1950. On the World War II basis of one mine in 40 being effective, such a total could, if cleverly used, sink or disable some 600 Western ships. Against that sort of arithmetic NATO's tardy program of mine countermeasures seems pitifully small.

8. AMPHIBIOUS WARFARE

The amphibious assault landing craft (AALC) known as JEFF-B, one of two prototypes built to develop an air cushion assault vessel for the US Navy.

The history of amphibious warfare ought to be as old as naval warfare itself, but surprisingly the need for it has been questioned in every generation. It has often been neglected, only to reassert its demands, and the relearning of its lessons has usually been both painful and expensive.

What military planners often overlook is the inescapable fact that a battle on the oceans by itself decides nothing. 'Command of the Sea' is a ringing term which all too often ignores the fact the sea is only a bridge between two land masses; without armies, a country cannot get to the enemy's heartland to bring the campaign to a conclusion. Extreme supporters of air power have tried to ignore both land power and sea power, claiming that 'Command of the Air' will be sufficient but as always, physical occupation of the objective is the only decisive outcome of a military campaign.

Modern amphibious doctrine stems directly from experience in World War II. After World War I, in which ideas on amphibious landings either failed or were so unambitious as to achieve only minor successes, both the Americans and the British developed doctrines to exploit the mobility conferred by command of the sea. As long ago as 1919 the Royal Marines started to discuss landing procedures and the type of Headquarters Staff organization which would be needed, followed by similar deliberations by the US Marine Corps. The US Marines got further because they were permitted to build experimental landing craft in sufficient numbers to make realistic exercises possible, but it was the British who found themselves at war first.

The development of amphibious warfare was a laborious process of trial and error, starting with a requirement from Winston Churchill that the British armed forces should hit back at Occupied Europe, to keep the German Army on the defensive, if for no better reason.

Although prototype vehicle landing craft had been built in small numbers the first tank landing craft were ordered just after the evacuation from Dunkirk in the summer of 1940. Two years later there was a sophisticated array of specialized craft available in sufficient numbers to permit the Dieppe Raid. That was a failure but it led the way to successful landings in North Africa, Sicily and mainland Italy. By June 1944 the Allies were ready for a gigantic operation, the Normandy Landings, during which 5000 ships and a million men would be deployed. Statistics become meaningless, but suffice it to say that some 130,000 men went ashore in the first 16 hours of the landings.

The use of amphibious techniques in the Pacific was even more dramatic. There the Japanese island garrisons were bypassed in a series of 'island-hopping' raids. Any island which appeared too tough a nut to crack was simply outflanked and left to wither on the vine. Even so, the dogged determination of the individual Japanese fighting man meant that each landing was enormously expensive in lives. The brunt of these operations was borne by the Marines, whose prewar exercises gave them at least the basis of a tactical doctrine for the task.

The *Fort Austin*, flagship of the Royal Fleet Auxiliary, one of the first ships to sail for the Falklands in 1982.

For the major Western navies and the US Navy in particular the clearest lesson from World War II was not only that amphibious warfare worked but that it was the *only* alternative to costly land fighting against the overwhelming numbers of the Soviet Army. Despite those exponents of air power and nuclear weapons, and even some jealousy from Army officers who resented the elite status of the Marine Corps, the US Navy maintained a strong amphibious element. Korea proved its need, when the Inchon landing enabled the UN forces to outflank the North Koreans

and throw them back on the defensive. During the 1950s and 1960s the role of the US Navy became increasingly one of crisis management, and for that purpose the amphibious element was absolutely essential.

The amphibious transports and specialized landing ships left over from World War II were replaced in the 1960s by a large modern assault force comprising a range of special units, each designed for specific missions. There were five groups of ships, of which the most flexible were the seven Amphibious Assault Ships (LPH) of the *Iwo Jima* class built in 1959–70. They are basically small helicopter carriers built to mercantile standards. Their task is to use their 20 large helicopters to land 2000 Marines, but since the introduction of the AV-8A Harrier ground support aircraft they have also been able to provide ground support when required. In appearance they are carriers, with small starboard islands, but they lack catapults and arrester wires.

The direct descendants of the wartime Dock Landing Ships were 14 Amphibious Transport Docks (LPDs) of the *Austin* and *Raleigh* classes, built between 1960 and 1971. They are capable of landing some 900 marines with their amphibious vehicles and landing craft, using a large floodable well-deck in the after part of the ship. They are in fact mobile floating docks, capable of closing the stern gate and pumping out the well for a normal sea passage. The benefit of having a docking well is that landing craft can be loaded in comparative safety, whereas landing craft alongside a conventional transport are at the mercy of the weather. Very similar to the LPDs are the five Dock Landing Ships (LSDs) of the *Anchorage* class, built in 1969–72. They carry more landing craft but at the expense of carrying only 400 marines.

Five Amphibious Cargo Ships (AKAs) of the *Charleston* class were built in 1966–70 to replace World War II conversions. They carry heavy equipment and supplies for an amphibious assault, as well

Bow and side views of the unique extending ramp of the US Navy's latest LSTs, the *Newport* class, the *Newport* herself being shown. This design was adopted to allow a normal ship bow form for higher speed.

as nine Landing Craft, Mechanized (LCMs) to get this material ashore. They are backed up by 20 Tank Landing Ships (LSTs) of the *Newport* class, built in 1966–72. Unlike World War II LSTs, the *Newport* and her sisters do not discharge their tanks and vehicles through bow doors. To meet a requirement for a speed of 20 knots they had to be given a conventional ship-shape forward, and so they discharge vehicles over a large hinged ramp.

To coordinate the diverse activities of these amphibious warfare ships two new Amphibious Command Ships (LCC) were built in 1967–71. Using the same hull as the *Iwo Jima* class LPH, the *Blue Ridge* and *Mount Whitney* provide command and communications facilities for the naval Commander Amphibious Task Group (CATG) and the Marine Landing Force Commander (LFC) and for their respective staffs.

In peacetime, replacement of amphibious ships comes quite low in priority, but ten *Whidbey Island* (LSD.41) class Dock Landing Ships are under construction. They would have been virtually repeats of the *Anchorage* class but the design was modified to embark two Air Cushion Landing Craft (LCACs). These are based on a prototype called JEFF-B, and an ultimate total of over 100 units is planned for completion during the next five years. Four each will be carried aboard the *Whidbey Island* class, and one aboard each of the *Tarawa* class assault ships. The US Navy is only following the lead given by the Soviets, who have exploited the unique qualities of hovercraft to cross over open beaches and move rapidly inland.

The amphibious warfare ships described usually operate in amphibious task forces built around the basic amphibious squadron, known as a PhibRon. Four of these PhibRons are normally assigned to the Pacific Fleet (two on forward deployment in the Western Pacific), and four to the Atlantic Fleet (one deployed forward in the Mediterranean). Their composition varies according to the Marine Amphibious Unit (MAU) embarked in each PhibRon, and according to the specific mission, so there can be no set size or standard list of equipment for a MAU. Typical figures, however, are 1600–2500 marines with tanks, amphibious tracked personnel carriers, artillery and lighter weapons, supported by 20–25 helicopters. A typical PhibRon is made up of an LPH, LPD, LSD and two LSTs, supported on forward deployments by an AKA, and they are all 20-knot ships.

This impressive group of ships is without equal in the world, but inevitably the US Marine Corps decided in the early 1970s that greater cost-effectiveness could be achieved by combining the functions of the various units of the PhibRon in a single hull. Of course the function of the LSTs could not be absorbed, for they must be able to beach, but it did prove possible to combine the functions of the LPH, LPD, LSD and AKA in a single LHA or amphibious assault

710

Above: HMS *Fearless*, one of two LPDs operated by the Royal Navy.
Left: Soviet amphibious forces make widespread use of assault hovercraft. Three classes, Gus, Lebed and Aist, are in service.

ship. The technical problems were daunting, for the designers had to combine vertical and horizontal movement of troops, as well as the flow of vehicles and supplies but the ships which resulted are impressive by any standard.

They combine a welldeck big enough to take the large utility landing craft with a full-length hangar high enough to take the biggest Marine Corps helicopters. They also stow and handle the heavy cargo of an AKA but without conventional mercantile holds and heavy-lift booms, and handle troops as efficiently as the specially-tailored LPD and LSD.

To fit a hangar above a large welldeck without excessive topweight called for a very big hull. The five *Tarawa* (LHA.1) class are 250 meters long, with a beam of 32.3 meters (just enough to get through the Panama Canal). At 39,300 tons full load they approximate to the Soviet cruiser/carrier *Kiev*, but whereas the Russian ship has a freeboard of 13 meters the *Tarawa*s have 18 meters. The difficulty of handling heavy cargo inside a part-carrier/part-floating dock hull required an ingenious application of mercantile containerization. This results in a unique ability to move cargo vertically by helicopter or horizontally by landing craft, and at the same time leave the flow of troops undisturbed. All the functions of the LPH, LPD, LSD and AKA have therefore been combined, but without interfering with one another.

The most visible feature of the *Tarawa* class is the flight deck, island and hangar, which gives the ships a superficial resemblance to carriers. The 65m × 30m × 8.5m hangar occupies the after part of the ship and is served by a side lift and a centerline lift right aft. The standard assault helicopter is the Boeing-Vertol CH-47 Sea Knight, which can carry 17–25 fully armed marines or 1350kg of cargo. In addition there are Sikorsky CH-53D Sea Stallions, capable of carrying 37 marines or 3600kg of cargo. It is currently being replaced by the bigger CH-53E Super Stallion, with a third engine; they can lift 14,600kg of cargo or 56 marines.

These heavy assault helicopters are backed up by the Bell AH-1 SeaCobra and the UH-1 Huey. The AH-1J version of the SeaCobra operates in the escort and defense suppression role, with a three-barreled 20mm gun, and the AH-1T can carry the TOW anti-tank missile. The 'Huey' is a utility helicopter used for command and control, or for casualty evacuation, in which role it can lift six stretcher patients and a medical orderly. The third element in the LHAs' air group is the AV-8A Harrier ground support aircraft, which is normally carried as a detachment of four, but sometimes expanded to as many as 22, if required. The unique Short TakeOff and Vertical Landing (STOVL) ability of the Harrier allows it to dispense with a catapult and arrester wires, and also eliminates the need for a heavily stressed flight deck, which would have added topweight.

The maximum stowage in the hangar is 30 helicopters, and the sight of a fully embarked air group in an LHA is a reminder that the figure of 30 is indeed a maximum. In peacetime the normal complement would be something like 12 Sea Knights, six Sea Stallions, four SeaCobras and two Hueys. Such an air group would have a lift capacity of 400–500 marines.

Underneath the hangar is the massive welldeck, 82 meters by 24 meters, divided lengthwise by a guide slip for the landing craft. Four big 41-meter *LCU.1610* class can be carried, each capable of lifting three M48 or M60 tanks. There are also two 22-meter LCM(6) landing craft, which can lift 80 troops or 34 tons of cargo; they are normally stowed on the flight deck and lifted into the water by crane. The LCUs can be loaded while the ship is underway, and when ready to

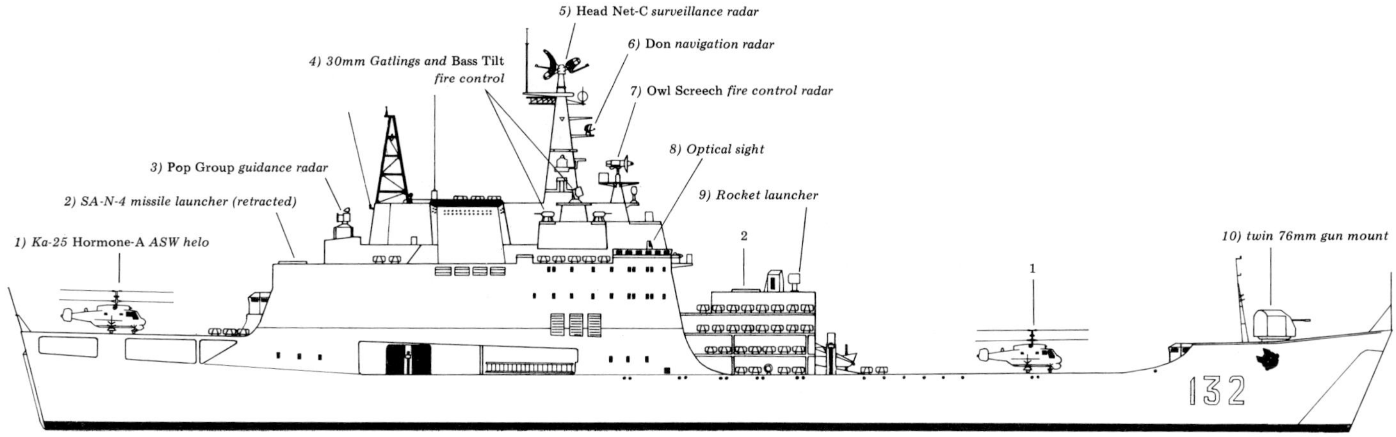

Top left and top right: The *Ivan Rogov* is the first of a new Soviet class of large assault ships equipped with a docking well aft as well as a conventional bow ramp.
Above: Small navies use tank landing ships for rapid movement of troops. This is the Nigerian *Ambe*, built in Germany.
Left: The USS *Spiegel Grove* (LSD.32) with an LCU about to enter her docking well.

disembark the dock is flooded, the ship keeping steady by using her bow-thruster. Once the LCUs are re-embarked the huge vertical sliding door makes the well watertight, allowing it to be pumped dry.

Vehicles and tanks are parked in a huge 'multi-story car park' containing 200 trucks, jeeps, tanks and LVTP-7 Amtrac armored personnel carriers. As the Amtracs are amphibious they swim out of the welldeck like the landing craft, and eight of them can be launched simultaneously. More than half the Marine Battalion can be landed by the Amtracs, as each one carries 25 marines.

Five LHAs were built in 1971–80, but the contract for the last four of the program was canceled in 1971 in spite of loud protests from the Marines. The cancellation has been felt keenly since then, especially as the five LHAs have proved an outstanding success. Their crews are proud of the versatility, and refer to the LHA as the 'ship that has everything'. Belated recognition of the error in not building all nine is implicit in the decision in 1982 to order a new class of LHD or helicopter/dock landing ships. They will have virtually the same hull as the LHA, but will emphasize more of the qualities of the LPD, by embarking a dozen LCM(6) and two LCACs, and 1800 marines.

It is interesting to contrast the Soviet Navy's approach to amphibious warfare, for although the Soviets have never achieved such a dazzling height of competence their Naval Infantry have a proud record of fighting on land, in contrast to a by and large dismal performance by the Navy during the Great Patriotic War. The later stages of that war saw considerable use of raids behind the German lines by small parties of troops, using small naval units to get in and out. Nor were all these landings small; over a hundred were made, involving 300,000 men, a remarkable feat when it is remembered that there were no specialized landing craft.

There was little incentive to develop highly specialized techniques of amphibious warfare, for unlike the US Navy which had to fight its way across the Pacific, the Russian Navy had to guard the flanks of the Red Army, either by evacuating cut-off detachments or using commando-style raids to secure bridgeheads during an advance. Amphibious forces were seen merely as adjuncts of land power, and despite its heroic record, the Naval Infantry was

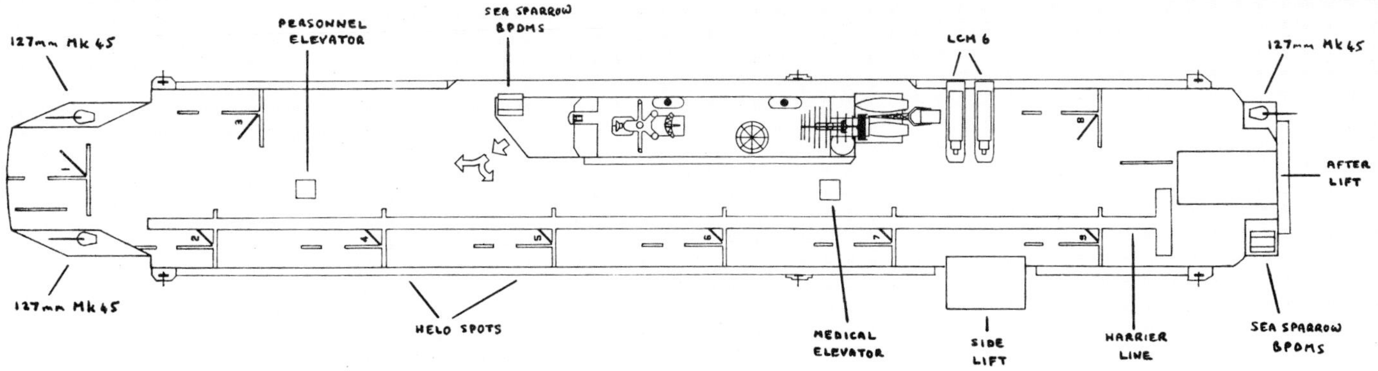

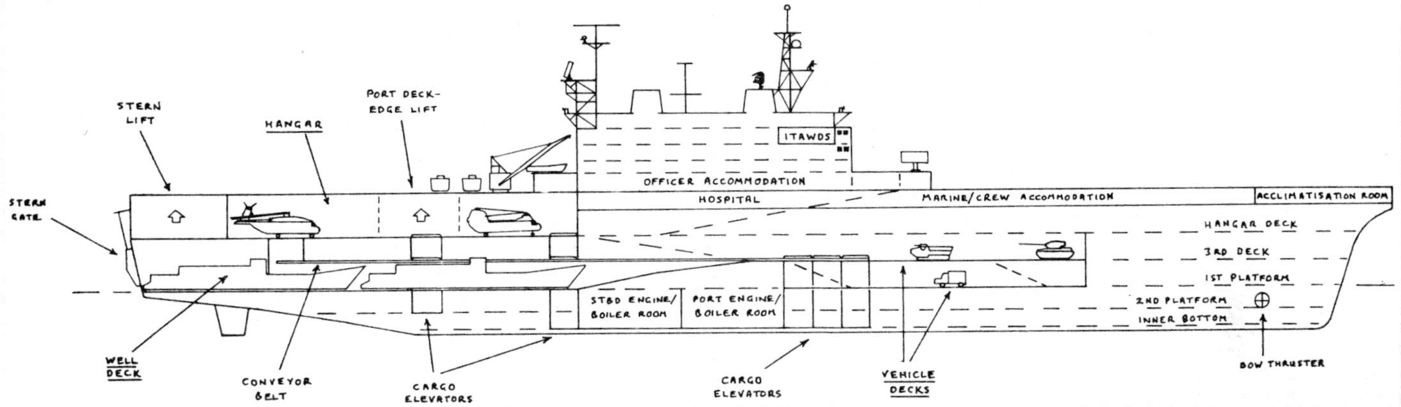

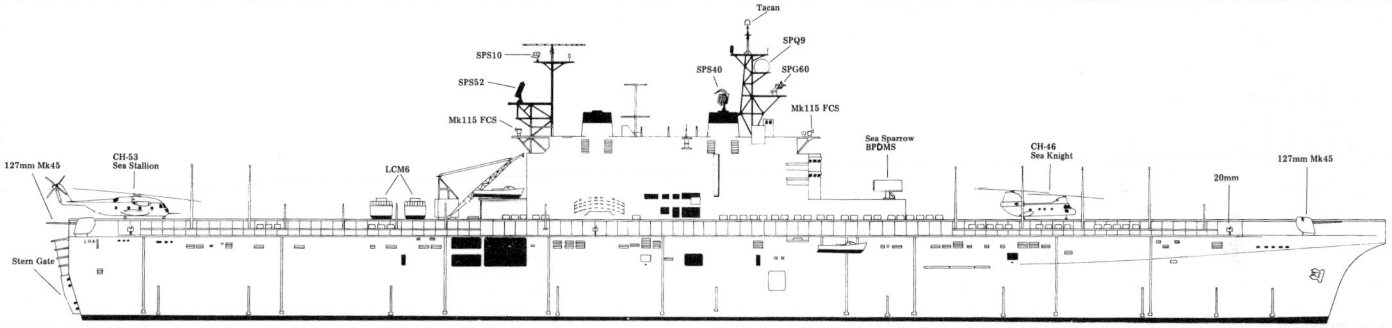

Above and left: The assault landing ships of the *Tarawa* class have an impressive multi-role capability with full-length flight decks and a docking well. At 40,000 tons they are as large as the Soviet *Kiev* class. *Tarawa* is shown at left.
Below: The assault ship USS *Inchon* (LPH.12) with Sea Knight and Sea Stallion transport helicopters on her flight deck.

disbanded after the war. Not until the 1960s, when the Soviets had seen numerous plans frustrated by British and American use of their amphibious forces, was the Naval Infantry reactivated. Since then several battalions have been allocated to each of the four fleets, with a Brigade HQ in each fleet. Current strength of the Naval Infantry is estimated at between 15,000 and 18,000 troops.

Several classes of small landing craft were built in the 1950s, but not until the following decade were specialized amphibious forces deployed in large numbers. From 1965 the Polish Stocznia Polnocny shipyard at Gdansk began to turn out a new type of LST, the Polnocny class. About 100 units were delivered, of which 65 were incorporated into the Soviet Navy, the remainder going to the Polish Navy and other friendly navies. They were a competent design, but hardly a match for their Western equivalents; they are roughly half the size of LSTs built in 1944–45.

About a year after the first Polnocny, a larger LST codenamed Alligator, appeared from a Russian shipyard. These 4000-ton LSTs are credited with lifting 20–25 vehicles and tanks and some 350–400 troops, and their high freeboard and diesel engines give them the ability to undertake long voyages. They have been seen off the coast of Africa and the Indian Ocean, and clearly gave the Soviet Navy a new capability for independent operations. The next LST to appear, the Ropucha class of 1975, seemed, however, to be an enlargement of the Polnocny design. Commentators see them as useful for 'local' amphibious operations in such areas as the Baltic, rather than in power-projection in support of foreign policy. All three classes carry a heavy defensive armament, 57mm guns in the Ropucha and Alligator classes and 30mm guns in the Polnocny class.

Surprisingly the Naval Infantry have not been given modern fighting vehicles, and the Soviet amphibious lift capability is correspondingly weak. The elderly T-54/55 tank is used, but it lacks the ability to 'swim' ashore. The PT-76 lightweight amphibious tank is capable of 'swimming' at a speed of 11 knots on its waterjets, but it has limited fighting value. The other standard fighting vehicle is the BTR-60 armored personnel carrier, which has better performance in water but poor land performance. It is being replaced by the BMP-1 Mechanized Infantry Combat Vehicle (MICV), which was introduced in 1967. It is better armored than the BTR-60 and is armed with a bigger gun as well as wire-guided anti-tank missiles, but carries fewer troops.

The next sign that Soviet ideas on amphibious warfare were becoming more ambitious was the appearance of a new LPD called *Ivan Rogov* in 1978. She is more than twice the displacement of any previous Russian amphibious ship, and is the first to have a docking well and a flight deck for helicopters. She displaces about 13,000 tons full load, is 158 meters long and has a bow door as well as a docking well in the stern. She is therefore built along traditional LST lines, with a continuous tank deck, unlike American and British LPDs.

When she first appeared Western commentators were inclined (as with all new Soviet designs) to ascribe remarkable qualities to her. A speed of at least 20 knots was suggested, putting her on a par with the latest American PhibRon ships. However it should be remembered that the *Newport* class LSTs had to adopt an unusual 'up-and-over' ramp in order to preserve a conventional fine bow form, otherwise they would not have been able to achieve 20 knots. As the *Ivan Rogov* has a bluff bow form with a beaching ramp behind double doors it is hard to see how she could achieve 20 knots without considerably more installed power than she is claimed to have.

Above: Mil Mi-8 Hip assault helicopters flying over fast strike craft of the Soviet Baltic Fleet during large-scale amphibious maneuvers.
Above left: A CH-46A Sea Knight helicopter on the flight deck of the carrier *John F. Kennedy*, closely observed by a Soviet Hormone.

Like previous amphibious warfare ships she is heavily armed, not only for self-defense but for shore bombardment. A twin 76mm gun mounting is sited on the forecastle, well positioned to support a landing as well as to defend the beachhead from air attack. Two pairs of 23mm 'Gatling' guns provide for close range defense, but there are also two SA-N-4 short range missile systems. For shore bombardment there is also a BM-21 artillery rocket launcher, similar to a system mounted in the Alligator class.

Authorities argue over the lift capacity of the ship. Some sources suggest two Gus type hovercraft, others say three Lebed type. A total of 700 troops seems very high, and is apparently based on the theory that it can embark two 350-man Naval Infantry battalions; the figure of 400 seems more reasonable if we are talking about the number of troops embarked for any length of time. Not even the Soviets, whose ideas on accommodation and personal comfort are perhaps less generous than Western navies', can expect to keep fighting men efficient by cooping them up in very cramped quarters.

The *Ivan Rogov* is clearly designed to operate her own helicopters, with a hangar built into the after superstructure. As many as six Kamov Ka-25 Hormone-A helicopters could be carried in this large hangar, but normally four are embarked. The Hormone can accommodate 12 soldiers on folding seats in the cabin, and if all six were embarked a total of 72 men could be lifted in a single sortie, but it may equally be possible that the ship is intended to act as a staging post for helicopters operated by other ships. What is certain is that the helicopter facilities are elaborate for such a small group – two separate flight decks, each with its own flying control position, plus large hangar doors and a ramp.

It seems likely that the *Ivan Rogov* is being evaluated to see just how she can fit into future amphibious warfare plans. The fact that she participated in a Baltic exercise before proceeding to the Far East on her first deployment lends support to this view. Subsequently exercises took place off East Africa, suggesting that no single role has been chosen, but she and a second ship which has not yet appeared are clearly intended to succeed the Alligator class in the furtherance of foreign policy. What should not be taken for granted, however, is that they are the spearhead of a massive incursion into the realm of offensive amphibious warfare. There are good reasons for thinking that the Soviet Navy is still tied to single-ship

1193

operations, and it is likely that the LPDs will not form part of a large amphibious warfare squadron. They are not particularly well equipped to provide command and control, by comparison with US Navy ships of similar type. They are on the large side for beaching, and carry no LCUs to take advantage of the docking well. On the other hand, the docking well is very small, and this restricts the number and type of air cushion vehicles and landing craft which can be embarked. Like the LHA, they are an attempt to combine a number of functions in one hull, but on only a third of the size, clearly the designers had to make compromises which have limited each function severely.

Most of the NATO and other Western navies operate small landing craft, but mainly for short range local operations. The only European navies to maintain a full amphibious capability are France and Great Britain. Each navy built two LPDs in the 1960s and a number of LSTs. The French *Orage* and *Ouragan* displace 8500 tons full load, whereas the British *Fearless* and *Intrepid* are about 50 percent larger, but both types lift about 350–400 troops. The French have built two medium-sized LSTs, the *Champlain* and *Francis Garnier*, known as the Batral type, and two more are under construction. To meet a similar peacetime need to move men, vehicles and supplies in peacetime the British Ministry of Transport in 1963 ordered six Logistic Landing Ships (LSLs) for the Army, 5600-ton ships resembling LSTs, with a bow and stern ramps for speedy movement of vehicles. In 1970 they were transferred to the Royal Fleet Auxiliary, the civilian-manned service which provides logistic support for the Royal Navy. Named after Knights of the Round Table, the *Sir Bedivere* class were built in 1965–67.

Left: The tank landing ship *Fairfax County* in company with the amphibious assault ship USS *Inchon*. The capabilities of both these ship types, as well as of the LPDs, are combined in one hull in the *Tarawa* class.
Right: The amphibious transport dock USS *Dubuque* (LPD.8), one of the US Navy's *Austin* class.
Main picture: A Sikorsky Sea Stallion heavy assault helicopter refuels from a KC-130 Hercules tanker. The US Marines have six Sea Stallion squadrons for their amphibious assault role.

Above: Two LCUs from HMS *Fearless* on her return from the Falklands. They carry Scorpion and Scimitar armored vehicles. Left: Soviet APCs and assault infantry coming ashore.

From 1966 it had been a cardinal principle of British defense policy that there would never be an occasion for British forces acting alone to make an opposed landing. It is therefore hardly surprising that apart from the Royal Marines, who kept the doctrine of 'amphibiosity' alive, British experience of beach assault has until recently been limited to a few days' exercising each year. The 'infrastructure', the civilian agencies in the dockyards, the ordnance depots and other departments which in the US Navy exist to support the PhibRons, had little or no opportunity to practise procedures. Certainly when Argentine forces invaded the Falkland Islands on Friday 2 April 1982 there was no blueprint for a campaign to be waged 8000 miles away from the United Kingdom.

Despite these inherent weaknesses, within a week of receiving mobilization orders the Reinforced 3rd Commando Brigade had sailed with sufficient of its War Materiel Reserve (WMR) for 30 days' land operations, as well as 60 days' specialist stores, and an additional 26 days' WMR to be kept in ships for resupply. In all 5000 tons of ammunition, rations and consumable stores, everything from missiles to clothing, was loaded into various LSLs and Royal Fleet Auxiliary supply ships, within 72 hours of the order to embark. By midday on Monday 5 April the ships were loaded and they sailed within 24 hours.

The work of planning this gigantic logistic operation was done by the Royal Marines' Brigade Staff and the staff of the Commando Logistic Regiment in Plymouth. An operations planning room was established, with a cell to prepare loading tables for individual units. This proved vital, for during that hectic weekend the situation regarding availability of shipping and composition of the Task Force was so fluid that it often altered while an officer was walking downstairs from the operations room to the loading cell. But in spite of all the difficulties final loading tables were complete by Monday.

As there are only 30 miles of good roads in the Falklands the decision was made to leave all wheeled vehicles behind. The risk was also foreseen that the small number of helicopters available might be immobilized by peat bogs if too many stores were sent ashore; the answer was to hold a floating reserve of stores.

To strengthen the hand of British diplomacy it was essential to get the amphibious force to sea as soon as possible. The Commodore Amphibious Warfare embarked in the LPD *Fearless*, while her sister *Intrepid* was hurriedly recommissioned. The flagship embarked both the Commodore's and the Marine Brigade's staffs, the Brigade's HQ and Signals Company, and some helicopter controllers. Many cargo ships were being requisitioned as storeships, but to get the maximum number of troops to the Falklands it was also necessary to requisition the 44,000-ton passenger liner SS *Canberra* – her new designation was

humorously styled as an LSLL or Landing Ship Luxury Liner. Later the *Queen Elizabeth II* was also used to carry 3000 men to the South Atlantic. During the voyage south there was time to plan the restowage of the ships, which had been very hurriedly loaded at Southampton. Once at Ascension Island there was also a chance to offer training and exercises for the troops. The period at Ascension gave time for the slower ships to catch up, and incidentally permitted the diplomats to make a last attempt at settling the dispute without fighting.

The landings at San Carlos on 21 May, seven weeks after the Argentine seizure followed a standard pattern: two LSLs supporting each assault, while helicopters lifted artillery and missiles ashore in the third phase. The simplicity of the plan was severely disrupted by the severe Argentine air raids; important ships had to be withdrawn. As the Brigadier had foreseen, air attacks disrupted movements of supplies, and helicopters supplying forward areas risked being shot down by Pucará ground-support aircraft. Not until the Navy Sea Harriers had begun to establish air superiority over the beachead and the Army's Rapier ground-to-air missile batteries were established ashore could the troops begin the break-out.

An example of how the loss of a key ship can prejudice an amphibious operation was the *Atlantic Conveyor*. This 15,000-ton roll on/roll off container ship was hit by two Exocet antiship missiles in an attack by two Argentine Navy Super Etendard strike aircraft on 25 May. She had taken RAF Harriers and Chinook heavy-lift helicopters down to the Falklands, as well as some 4000 tons of vital stores, including a portable airstrip, refueling gear and aircraft bombs. She had previously flown off the Harriers but three of the four Chinooks were lost, along with a Lynx, and six Wessex helicopters. The Chinooks, each capable of lifting 12 tons (four times the load of a Sea King) were sorely missed ashore. As a direct result, the LSLs had to shoulder a greater burden, resupplying forward units of the land forces.

The six LSLs proved invaluable, but could not be risked freely as they were so lightly defended. Just how vulnerable they were was proved dramatically on 8 June, when Argentine aircraft caught the LSLs *Sir Galahad* and *Sir Tristram* in Bluff Cove, to the South East of East Falkland. Both ships were quickly set on fire, and as a large number of troops were still on board the casualties were comparatively high – 43 Welsh Guards killed and many badly burned. It was

Above: USMC AV-8A Harriers are used in the ground support role and can operate from attack carriers or assault ships.
Top right: The *Queen Elizabeth II* seen off South Georgia during the Falklands Conflict.

a scene familiar to any veteran of Normandy or the big landings in the Pacific, but under the full glare of TV cameras it took on the appearance of a disaster. In fact neither LSL was sunk, and the rough handling of the Welsh Guards caused no delay in the surrender of the Argentine forces six days later.

Despite the hostile terrain, the bitterly cold weather, the shortage of helicopters and the persistent air attacks, the British won the logistic battle in the Falklands. An ultimate total of 8000 tons of supplies was taken ashore. The Commander Land Forces could rest content that his men had not only outfought the enemy but also out-thought him. The axis of the amphibious assault was deliberately East-West because it was likely to catch the Argentine defenders unprepared. It was reasoned that General Menendez and his staff would at least have read US Marine Corps manuals on amphibious warfare, even if they had not been trained by Marines. So a plan of attack was chosen which was contrary to US practice. Thus instead of a direct assault over the beaches near Port Stanley, followed by a drive for the most useable roads, the British landed at the other end of the island, and then took the defenders in the rear; most of the defences around Port Stanley were found to be sited on a North-South axis, instead of East-West, proof that General Moore's strategy was well-founded.

Before the Falklands Campaign the Royal Navy had been under strong pressure to abandon its amphibious capability. The LPDs were to be scrapped (HMS *Intrepid* had even been offered to Argentina), the LSLs were to go, and there was even talk of disbanding the Royal Marines. Since 1982 the scene looks different; two roll on/roll off ships have been chartered to replace the LSLs (*Sir Galahad* was scuttled but *Sir Tristram* was salvaged and taken back to the United Kingdom). To resupply the Falklands garrison a North Sea ferry has been bought, and is now in service as the troop transport HMS *Keren*. The future of British amphibious forces is not clear, but what has been demonstrated is that without even the limited capability possessed in 1982 the Falklands operation could not have been contemplated.

If a government needs to project power beyond its shores, there is very little alternative. With only a short runway at Port Stanley it was not possible to fly in reinforcements, so the small garrison was overwhelmed. Even if a long runway capable of taking large military transport aircraft had existed, a surprise attack could capture it before reinforcements arrived. Once hostile forces were in occupation there remained only one option to the British, an amphibious assault. The other option, an attack on mainland Argentina was simply not feasible. What applied in the South Atlantic applies elsewhere; despite the advances in air transport heavy equipment has to be moved by sea, and heavily armed troops have to be put ashore from ships. But, even more important is the fact that the complexities of amphibious warfare have to be entrusted to specially trained soldiers, such as the US Marines and the Royal Marines – amphibiosity is certainly not a doctrine which can be hurriedly imbibed.

9. PROSPECTS FOR THE FUTURE

It is now generally admitted that World War III is unlikely to be started by a massive Warsaw Pact assault on NATO's Central Front. What is much more feasible is a confrontation at sea, brought about by the maneuvering of rival fleets during a time of tension in, say, the Middle East. Given more involvement by the Superpowers even a minor fracas like the Anglo-Argentine conflict in the Falklands could have precipitated a major clash.

Confrontation at sea has many attractions to an aggressor. Nuclear weapons could be used with a greatly reduced risk of massive retaliation, for example. Sad as it is to admit it, public opinion would probably accept the deaths of several hundred sailors in the North Atlantic whereas the threat of nuclear weapons being used on land is likely to produce widespread panic among the civilian populace. Scenario-writing is a favorite pastime for defense commentators and uniformed servicemen, and it is not difficult to imagine situations which could lead to an inadvertent clash of arms.

Tension could arise directly between the Soviet Union and a NATO country such as Denmark or Norway, over fishery rights, or it could arise from Russian intervention in a dispute between two other countries. Although few would have predicted a violent shooting war between Britain and Argentina over the Falklands, once that war had broken out, there was plenty of reason to think that Argentina would turn to the Soviet Union for direct or indirect help. It is not long since the Western nations had to watch impotently while Soviet ships carried 10,000 Cuban soldiers from the Caribbean to Angola. In both instances, the other Superpower had the military means to intervene but judged the risks to be too great. What might have happened if the Soviet Union had tried to frighten the British Task Force away from the Falklands or the US Navy had tried to prevent the Cubans from reaching Angola can be imagined all too easily, and the consequences are incalculable.

In today's world a lack of respect for International Law has become endemic, but notably among small nations, many of whom possess impressive armories of Western or Soviet weapons. The chronic instability of their governments, combined with the lethality of their weaponry makes for an explosive combination. Most leaders of such countries forget that even the Superpowers can run out of patience, particularly when national pride is being openly humiliated. During the final stages of the Tehran Hostages crisis in 1980 the loss of American patience was noticeable.

There were rumors of Soviet intervention, and they, combined with the possibility of kamikaze-type attacks on US ships in the Arabian Gulf, made for an inclination to 'shoot first and ask questions afterward'. Foreign warships operating in the Gulf in support of the Americans were well aware of the need to identify themselves very clearly to US Navy ships, and had any attempt been made to kill the US Embassy hostages there would have been massive reprisals against Iran. Fortunately on that occasion the nearest Soviet forces were very weak, and they were wisely kept out of the way.

The front-line navies of the West accordingly find themselves performing a police role very similar to the 'Gunboat Diplomacy' role of the Royal Navy in the 19th Century. The difference is that the gunboats are bigger and the natives are better armed. With so many high quality weapons in various hands, ships are liable to be attacked by the most capable missiles, against which they must have the most sophisticated defenses if they are to survive. The name of the game is 'crisis-management', but the concept of a flag-carrying 'gunboat' has no place in today's peacekeeping. The high stakes are played for with appropriately high value cards.

Navies face another problem familiar to the 19th Century scene, an explosion of technology without sufficient practical experience to give clear guidance on the future. The Vietnam War was very specialized, and like the fighting between Arabs and Israelis, occurred more than a decade ago. The fighting in the South Atlantic was also specialized, and it would be all too easy to make incorrect deductions. In fact the biggest risk at the moment is that the Anglo-Argentine War will provide false analogies, in much the same way that the Crimean War and the Battle of Lissa misled a generation of naval tacticians and theorists.

Of one thing we can be certain: more attention will be paid to defeating the sea-skimming missile, whether by electronic warfare or by point-defense systems. Another certainty is that antisubmarine warfare will be given top priority. It remains to be seen if towed arrays will achieve the long-sought breakthrough in combating the menace of the submarine, but as always, the fallacy of the 'dominant weapon' should be borne in mind. There has never been a weapon to which there is no antidote, and the more menacing it appears the more effort will be devoted to countering it. Even the intercontinental ballistic missile may lose its aura of invincibility in the next generation, and there is talk of harnessing blue-green lasers in the antisubmarine war.

In the line-up of new warships paraded in previous chapters it is perhaps surprising that so few 'unconventional' craft are to be found. Comparatively few hydrofoils and hovercraft are in service, and then only in ancillary roles; even the missile hydrofoils are only reinforcements for large numbers of more traditional 'displacement hulls'. There is certainly no sign of the hover-frigates and large hydrofoils which were so

Left: The nuclear-powered guided missile cruiser USS *Bainbridge* (CGN.25).
Below: A Soviet *Moskva* class helicopter carrier operating a variable depth sonar installation over her stern.

confidently predicted 20 years ago. Even the most promising idea, the SWATH (Small Waterplane Area, Twin Hull) has only reached the prototype stage. The hovercraft has been tried out in a number of military roles, but apart from the mine countermeasures task, mentioned earlier, it has proved to have too many drawbacks. Its cousin, the rigid sidewall surface effect ship, shows more promise, but also suffers from poor performance in rough weather.

The hydrofoil, like other unconventional hulls is much more expensive ton-for-ton than an equivalent warship, and it is a poor payload-lifter. Studies suggest an upper limit of 3000–4000 tons, but the cost has so far proved prohibitive, and nothing has come of various plans.

The SWATH offers not only higher speeds but significant improvements to seakeeping. Its large semi-catamaran hull is exceptionally steady in a seaway, and even on 200 tons the US Navy's prototype *Kaimalino* operates a helicopter. Although it shares the drawback of the hydrofoil and hovercraft, not being able to support extra-heavy loads, it can tolerate a great deal of extra topweight. Most SWATH designs are based on two sets of tall struts surmounting a pair of fully submerged torpedo-like hulls containing the propulsion units.

The hull form has an underwater area much greater than a conventional hull of similar tonnage, and so requires more power to achieve cruising speed. However, once over a hump speed of about 25–35 knots efficiency improves considerably. The real advantage is shown in rough weather; there is virtually no loss of speed in head seas, as compared with, say, a destroyer, which would need some 15 percent more power to maintain a speed of 30 knots.

What has been holding up development of the SWATH is the technical difficulty of squeezing a large amount of power into the small underwater hulls. It is possible to put the engines in the above water portions of the hull, but that would involve great difficulty in transmitting the drive down to the submerged bodies. It will also be a difficult ship to dock, because of its great draught and beam; one solution suggested is to lighten the SWATH in harbor and then ballast down when at sea.

What makes the SWATH tempting in a military configuration is the fact that it could be built easily in non-specialist shipyards, or even well away from shipyards. Also the very large area of deck lends itself to helicopter flying, vertically-launched missiles, or modular weapons. The most likely SWATH ship may end up as 15,000–20,000 tons, but not more. Over that size she would be outclassed by conventional ships in seakeeping, and the problems of docking would be insuperable.

The changes in weaponry are not too difficult to predict. Existing missiles are likely to be repackaged, particularly for vertical launch. Vertical launching, once it is proven, will undoubtedly dictate some changes in the layout of warships. The next generations of warships are likely to have their superstructures configured with vertical launch systems in mind, whereas today's ships have been designed with conventional launchers and magazines in mind. Guns are already back in favor, after two decades of oblivion, but we are not likely to see a return to the large caliber guns with high rates of fire that were designed during and after World War II. Instead we will see small (20–40mm) multibarrel guns used as point-defense against missiles, and medium-caliber (3inch–8inch) guns in unmanned but comparatively slow-firing mountings. The missile lobby was successful in killing off the 8inch lightweight gun for the US Navy, but some similar idea may emerge. The British, after ruling out even a single 4.5inch gun for their frigates are now redesigning the later *Broadsword* class to get the gun back in. During the Falklands War some 8000 round of 4.5inch ammunition were fired – in a campaign of only 14 weeks' duration; and the US Marines are no longer alone in their demand for more firepower.

The antiship missile is likely to become faster. At present they are subsonic, but clearly a supersonic approach will cause the defense even more problems of reaction time than it has now. The guidance systems are also getting clever, adopting a variety of maneuvers during the approach; this also complicates the task of the defensive systems. As always the electronic war means that warheads become resistant to one form of jamming, but the jamming then becomes smarter in turn.

Many fears have been expressed about reliability of all the complex electronics in modern warships. This has been worrying designers as well, and modern equipment is intended to be more reliable. During the Falklands War an amazingly high degree of maintenance was achieved, and even equipment normally replaced rather than repaired (ie there were no repair manuals kept on board) was kept working by repairing or even creating new spare parts. In two instances toasters were 'cannibalized' to provide spares for electronic equipment. Machinery also exceeded expectations, and no machinery breakdown forced the withdrawal of any ship – contrary to a claimed forecast by the Commander-in-Chief of the Armada Republica Argentina that the British ships would break down before they reached the South Atlantic.

Twenty-five years ago it was fashionable to predict that navies were on the way out, and that such naval forces as existed in the 1980s would be adjuncts of the Air Force. Nobody looking at the extraordinary array of warships presently coming into service or being planned would take that sort of prophecy seriously. Warships and sea power are as important today as they were in 1945, and the loss of sea control by the West could never be counterbalanced by gains on land or in the air.

INDEX

Page numbers in italics refer to illustrations

Acknowledgments

The author and publishers would like to thank Adrian Hodgkins who designed this book and Ron Watson who prepared the index. The following agencies and individuals kindly supplied the illustrations on the pages noted.

Belgian Armed Forces: p 9 top
Bison Picture Library: pp 19 top, 52 left
Blohm & Voss: pp 150–151
Bremer Vulcan: pp 124–125 bottom
British Aerospace: pp 21 top, 83 lower, 97 lower, 186–187
Bundesmarine: pp 48, 60–61 top, 111 top
Cantieri Navale Breda: pp 75, 134–135
Danish Navy: p 69 bottom
Dassault Breguet: pp 94–95, 149 top
ECPA: pp 16 top, 34, 40–41, 50, 82, 93, 96, 111 bottom, 147
Empresa Naçional Bazán: pp 54–55
General Dynamics: pp 30–31, 42–43, 47
Goodyear Aerospace: pp 58–59
V. Graham: pp 154–155
Italian Navy: pp 103, 117
Japanese Maritime Self Defense Force: pp 9 lower, 133
John Jordan (artwork): pp 177, 179
Mike Lennon: pp 107 both inset, 128, 177 lower
McDonnell Douglas: pp 24 top, 83 top, 129
Ministry of Defence, London: pp 26–27, 36–37, 73, 85 top, 116, 130 top, 148 top, 156–157, 160, 174–175, 187 top right
MoD via MARS: p 78
Nippon Steel Tube: pp 164–165
Norwegian Navy: p 74 top
Novosti: p 189
OTO Melara: p 119 top right
Plessey Marine: p 118
PPL: pp 22 bottom left, 38 both, 46, 52–53, 60 bottom, 65, 69 top, 74 bottom 76–77, 84, 112, 114, bottom, 139 top, 159 bottom, 184
John Roberts (artwork): 46–47, 86–87, 142–143
via Rolls-Royce: p 15 bottom
SAAB-Scania: p 68 top
Scott Lithgow: pp 50–51
Sikorsky: pp 1, 126–127, 151 top left, 158–159 top
Société ECA: p 158 top left
Swan Hunter: pp 122–123
TASS: p 174 bottom
C & S Taylor: pp 12–13, 24–25, bottom, 56–57, 88–89, 98–99, 106–107, 113, 162–163, 170–171, 185
Thomson CSF: p 11 inset
US Marine Corps: p 178
US Navy: pp 2–3, 8–9, 10 both inset, 10–11, 14, 15 top, 16 bottom, 17 top, 18–19, 20 both, 21 bottom, 22–23 except bottom left, 28, 29, 30, 31, 32 all three, 35 both, 39, 44–45 all three, 49, 54 bottom, 60 center, 62–63, 66–67 all three, 68 bottom, 70–71 all four, 72, 79, 80 both, 85 bottom, 86–87 lower two, 90–91 all three, 92 both, 95 top, 97 top, 100–101, 104 both, 105, 108–109, 114–115 top, 115, 119 bottom, 120–121 all three, 122 top, 123 top, 124–125 top, 130–131, 136 top, 138–139, 140–141, 142–143 lower three, 145 both, 148–149, 151 top right, 152–153 both, 161 both, 168–169, 172, 173, 176 both, 177 bottom, 180, 182 top, 183 inset, 188
Vickers: pp 4–5, 119 top left
William J Welch: pp 136–137
Westland Helicopters: p 146
World Wide Photos: p 181
Yarrow Shipbuilders: pp 6–7, 17 bottom, 18 top, 25 top
Jacket pictures: all US Navy except *Swiftsure* class submarine (John Roberts) and HMS *Birmingham* (MoD via MARS).